Authentic Victorian Villas and Cottages

DESIGNED FOR THE CAPITOL OF ILLINOIS.

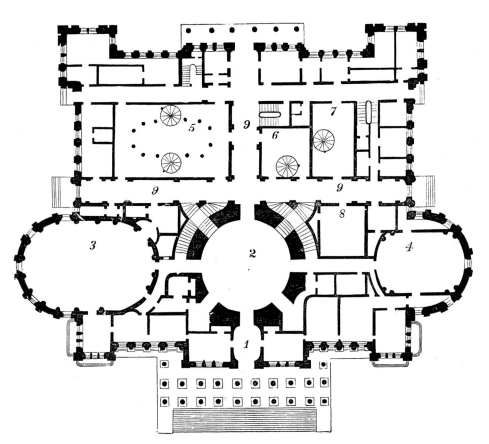

PLAN OF THE PRINCIPAL FLOOR OF OUR DESIGN FOR ILLINOIS STATE CAPITOL.

2. GRAND ROTUNDA.   3. HALL OF REPRESENTATIVES.   4. SENATE CHAMBER.

Authentic Victorian Villas and Cottages

OVER 100 DESIGNS WITH ELEVATIONS AND FLOOR PLANS

Isaac Hobbs

DOVER PUBLICATIONS, INC.
Mineola, New York

Bibliographical Note

This Dover edition, first published in 2005, is an unabridged republication of the second edition—revised and enlarged—of the work originally published in 1876 by J. B. Lippincott & Co., Philadelphia, under the title *Hobbs's Architecture: Containing Designs and Ground Plans for Villas, Cottages, and Other Edifices, Both Suburban and Rural, Adapted to the United States.*

Library of Congress Cataloging-in-Publication Data

Isaac H. Hobbs and Son.
    [Hobbs's architecture]
    Authentic Victorian villas and cottages : over 100 designs with elevations and floor plans / Isaac Hobbs.
       p. cm.
    Unabridged republication of: Hobbs's architecture. 2nd ed., rev. and enl. Philadelphia : Lippincott, 1876.
    ISBN 0-486-44351-5 (pbk.)
    1. Architecture, Domestic—United States—Designs and plans. 2. Architecture, Victorian—United States—Designs and plans. 3. Architecture—United States—19th century—Designs and plans. I. Title.

NA7207.H59 2005
728'.37'0973—dc22

2005049688

Manufactured in the United States of America
Dover Publications, Inc., 31 East 2nd Street, Mineola, N.Y. 11501

TO THE MANY

LADIES THROUGHOUT THE UNITED STATES

WHO HAVE FOR YEARS AIDED US BY THEIR SUGGESTIONS IN
PREPARING MANY OF THE MOST PRACTICAL AND BEAU-
TIFUL GROUND PLANS FOUND IN THIS VOLUME,

IT IS RESPECTFULLY AND AFFECTIONATELY

DEDICATED.

CONTENTS.

8   *CONTENTS.*

INTRODUCTION.

I SHALL commence my remarks by asking the question, What is architecture? and endeavor to answer the same. According to Webster, it is "building according to the science or the art of building, performed by the architect or master-builder:" simply this, and nothing more. A builder, therefore, who designs at all, is an architect, and any building that is erected is architecture. So much for authority.

Good architecture consists in three things: Fitness, Design, and Mechanism. If any one of these particulars is faulty, the architect is responsible; holding, as he does, the position of umpire, it is possible for him to obtain them, and impossible for any other person connected with a building.

By Fitness, is meant that the building or work has the quality of subserving in the best manner according to the positive knowledge of its needs possible to obtain when built, or, in other words, arranging the various parts in such a manner that the least possible amount of labor to fulfill the various offices needed in the working of the structure, in such a manner that the building may be fully adapted to perform all that it is intended for.

The requirements of a theatre, for instance, are, that all the audience shall see and be able to hear with distinctness; that it shall be properly heated in winter, cooled in summer, and ventilated properly and thoroughly in all seasons; direct and easy means of ingress and exit should be provided; the stage also should be so arranged that all the working parts should be the most convenient possible; the building should be fitted to the size and wants of the town, and be adapted to the climate and habits of the people. All these and many more facts must be taken into consideration, weighed, and, in a word, governed by good sense.

(9)

Fitness must be considered as a general common sense that must pervade the work in order that every part may be balanced, and not, as is frequently the case, one part be over-large and another meanly small. The only means of acquiring this branch of architecture is by observation and learning to think clearly, I might say, mechanically. Endeavor to avoid that general view which most people take of that which surrounds them. A head full of half-understood matter, for an architect, is no head at all. In order that an individual may discover to what amount he comprehends what he sees, let him look at any object for some time until he thinks he understands it; then as a test let him shut his eyes, bring upon his imagination the image, and contemplate it in this manner for a time, until he examines thoroughly all his understanding has received; then, upon opening his eyes and looking again upon the object, he will begin correctly to estimate his powers of perception, and, if they are defective, try to improve them by practice, examination, study of principles, and gathering of details, day after day, and so improve a dull understanding that in a short time, by a mental gymnastic process of this kind, the eyes will be able to afford architectural abilities rapidly to the student. I often think that good judgment is as capable of being taught as mathematics, philosophy, or anything else. Yet how often do we meet gentlemen possessed of excellent education, with miserably cultivated judgment; it will, in most cases, be traceable to the want of a cultivated perception founded upon a correct understanding. I do not know of anything more capable of cultivating the mind than drawing from sketches made from nature by the person drawing,—a practice I cannot too strongly recommend to every student of architecture, as nothing will more rapidly test your understanding than drawing it from memory.

Proportion—I mean in an artistic sense of the word—is playing, as it were, tunes with angles, curves, and lines in such a manner that they will at once impress the eye and judgment of the beholder with the sentiment you wish awakened, be it grave or sad, loveliness, gayety, or frivolity, grand or beautiful, be it in harmony with the surging cataract, or the peaceful lawn and sylvan retreat; is devotion to speak in its lines, or the empty laugh of a clown. Tunes can be played with lines as well as sounds; harmony and discord are alike with both: the only difference is that music demands the memory to link the note sounded with what was sounded before. With lines, all is before you. Madame De Staël defines architecture to be "frozen music." It is crystallized sentiment; and where its keys are touched by master-hands like the Greeks, its tone is chaste solemnity; by the Gothic fathers, reverential devotion; by the Egyptian, awful grandeur.

In designs there are four principal lines: the horizontal, the vertical, the diagonal, and the curved. The horizontal is the grand and strong line; the vertical, the sublime line; the diagonal, the rustic or indefinite line, changing towards the character of the two lines horizontal and vertical. When nearly horizontal, as in the Greek pediment, it becomes somewhat grand; and when bearing towards the perpendicular, as in the Gothic, it is on the track to the sublime, as attested by the Gothic spires and lofty gables of the early English architecture.

These four lines should be studied carefully. Ample opportunity for study of the horizontal is afforded in the Egyptian and Grecian, and in bridges; the vertical in the Gothic, as the sublime predominates in that style. There is character in forms. The ovoid or egg form is the most beautiful and varied of all forms, the circle for grace, the polygon for plainness.

In further illustration of these principles, permit me to direct you, for the first, to the human face. The nearer it approximates to the ovoid, the more beautiful and rounded it becomes; the more angular, the plainer, as is fully demonstrated by Harding in his beautiful work on art.

Now with the three lines described, and the three forms, by an harmonious evolution of them, tunes can be played, and are played by the Great Controller of things. The human countenance attests. The frown, the smile, the hope, the fear, the cunning, and the craft are all displayed upon so small a work as the human face, and so plainly are they written there that the child sees and feels them. I would therefore advise the student of architecture to look for his models of style and character to the human form. There he will find scope for all the genius he has or possibly can attain. The outlines of a beautiful human form are so exquisitely fine that nothing can excel them: the tapering of a finger, the beautiful curves of the various muscles, the refined balance of quantities throughout, the delicate but beautiful contrasts, every part uniting with others by a beautiful evolution of lines and quantities. Being thoroughly schooled by such a master, like the Grecians, you too may defy the criticism of ages, and stand proudly forward, admired and imitated. The statue of an Apollo, or a Venus, or a Hercules, etc., will be of great aid to the student of architecture. Learn to appreciate their beauties, and obtain a feeling for the slight but beautiful varying curves; see the effect that one part has upon another, and learn the great truth, that harmony is the cause of beauty. Contrasts are to be used simply as accessories, in order to make them felt. How many miss in this principle! Artists, architects, and others who fritter away all the beauty by disjointed contrasts, rendering weak and puerile that which should be whole and grand. Do not imagine that I want a humdrum style. No; I desire variety. Variety of form, in quantity, in appliances of every kind to produce it. Let the lightning flash, the thunder roll, the waves heave. Let them all co-operate, and for a while be as one, until the strongest force becomes master and leads the whole, aiding, by the murmurs of the others, the positive voice of the leading spirit.

There are many persons who are so constituted that they do not care for music; there are those also who have no eye for the appreciation of beautiful forms. There is no excuse for ugly features to build up architectural subjects but bad proportion. Place a statue upon your architecture, as did the Greeks; if it harmonizes, the architecture is good, but if the grotesque alone can harmonize with your work, you have not reached the highest refinement. It is like placing fine cloth alongside of that which is coarse—you see at once the fineness of the one and the coarseness of the other. Two blacks may, to the untutored eye, appear the same; but take an equal quantity of white lead and mix with each, and you immediately see a marked difference in the different lead-colors produced. Place a well-proportioned building in a row of guessed-at ones, and you will see a marked defect in what you previously deemed good architecture. They are too frequently made up by the hard blows and long rubbings of the artisans. A piece of white marble, a perfect cube,—the worst possible shape to be regular,—will be beautiful if finely polished, with smooth faces and square sides. Yet how often do we pass buildings of that material without noticing them! What has become of the artistic skill, the fine material? It has been sacrificed to bad proportion; its solidity and enduring grandeur have been sacrificed. How much carving is thrown away, having no force at all, simply for want of good proportion. Every one appreciates a beautiful horse, dog, or other animal; and it is the same with architecture: you have not the beauty, or you would gaze upon the silent music with emotions of delight. We want architecture to appear what it costs; if expensive material, you must have graceful forms, properly adjusted; if the beauty of the materials exceeds the genius of the design, then it is lost, and the whole sinks into monotonous contempt. The purer the materials, the more exact must be the proportion, or the one will neutralize the other and spoil the effect. Architects should be chosen by their merit, and not by favor, which is mostly done; those who will succeed in getting them must buy the job. It is a disgrace to the age that large, important, modern buildings have so little architectural merit; the good taste of the age is slandered to build the outrageous trash that is constantly being thrown up in Philadelphia and other cities, without proportion or good judgment. I could enumerate hundreds of absolute failures in design and effect, when contrasted with their cost,—works of such proportion that their size alone should make them grand.

As I have found so much fault with bad proportion, perhaps it will be expected of me to enlighten the community upon the subject,—which was not the intention of this work, but merely to give a reprint of my designs published in *Godey's Ladies' Book*, with a few others prepared especially for the present volume. We have a law of architectural proportion, discovered by us ten years ago, which I have found unfailing in designing and executing work; giving our buildings, wherever carried out, a fullness and beauty of proportion found nowhere save among the Greek examples. With it, the Mansard-roof ceases to be boxlike in appearance, and houses have the appearance of being worth twice or three times their cost.

I am fully impressed with the idea that the Greeks who built the Parthenon had the same law to guide them that we pursue, instead of the law given by Vitruvius having governed them, which in truth is no law at all, but the results of measurements made by a rule formed from the diameter of the columns at their bases, called modules,—a happy process for copying, but nothing more; like an artist, who, when he wishes to copy a picture, fills it with a number of squares of equal size, and makes the same number upon the sheet on which he is to copy. If he wishes to enlarge it, he makes the squares larger; if he wishes it smaller, he makes the squares less. A law, if I understand the term aright, must be something which, by an evolution of its principles, obtains a positive result, or a mathematical reality.

The more I examine the works of Greece in the ruins of Athens and other places, the more do I find that all buildings, though different in proportion of parts, are in their evolutions traceable to a decided law: every stone has a length and breadth founded upon the same principle as the diameter of the columns, height of pediment, intercolumniations, and every other part of the building.

A general principle must run throughout every design, to be good; if not, it will be like an artist's picture without an atmosphere. It may be a laborious assembly of details, but have a mechanical stiffness, a cold barrenness, admired by no person of cultivation and taste.

The proportion of a doorway will afford an example of the means I make use of. Now, as a doorway is for man to walk through, its best proportion will be found in a well-developed man. We will take a man as six feet high, and eighteen inches broad across the shoulders; if we make the door three feet wide, it will be just double his width,—that is, standing in the middle, he will have just nine inches of clear space on each side of him. If the same is given for the top, above the head, it will be six feet nine inches, making the opening three feet by six feet nine inches, —a very usual and beautiful size for doors. Now, if we find that this measurement neither looks high nor low, but right, we have a standard to work from. When we wish to increase the apparent width of a room, we increase the height of doors, or make them narrower; if we wish to increase the height, we make them wider. Just as a painter works with his pigments: if he wishes a tone to look blue, he brings orange in contrast; if red, he brings green. The effects in architecture are the same. It is not the colors you see in a picture that render it beautiful, but the effect produced upon the eye and senses. It is so with the proportions of houses, rooms, etc.: we do not let you see yellow, lake, and gamboge, but effects of air, water, trees, etc. Conventionalities may compel certain sizes, but genius by accessories can make them appear what it desires; the low can be thrown aloft, the high brought down, the wide narrowed, and all can have, by artistic arrangement, a mysterious effect pervading the whole, and thus with quiet eloquence speak with the soul of architecture. The Greeks understood this law, and gave their columns their entasis or swelling form in the centre, the effect that would be in nature as a person stands and looks upon a column or shaft : the lower part, as high as the level of the eye, the nearest point ; the next foot up the shaft will be a little farther off; the higher you look up the column, the distance increases in greater ratio ; and, by applying the law of perspective, that objects decrease in size according to the square of the distance, you have the parabolic curve of the Grecian entasis.

Yet this must be gently done, to give apparent height to the pillars. If overdone, as abundant samples will testify all over the land where they have been used, their effect of height is gone, and down comes their height ; as the sham is obvious, the effect is entirely reversed. This is also true in painting : for instance, a blue will recede until it becomes noticeable as blue, then it comes forward in your picture. All effects, properly made, tell with force and energy ; overdone, they show their poverty by utterly destroying, and are worse than nothing.

Ignorant people often think that they can collect beautiful parts of one building and transfer them to others, and have the same effect. So they could, if they knew how to balance their proportion and adapt them to the new situation thoroughly; but if not, they will fail, as can be seen everywhere in town and country. A handsome cornice upon one house may be an extravagant abortion upon another. I would therefore advise the study of proportion by all.

I would advise all to look to the human face and form, where character dwells, and study it : the smiling face, with all the muscles curling up; the saddened countenance, tending down, like the weeping willow and every drooping thing in nature. Study that, the fountain wherefrom all things start; it will lead to higher thoughts, and you will obtain a more noble future than by copying.

What I have said has been upon the soul of architecture,—that part which lives forever, and has immortal life.

Let me now descend to the mechanical part,—that which takes

upon itself to so balance quantities that they produce strong, enduring, and rational edifices, with constructions fully adequate to their wants.   In the first place, we take into consideration the materials of which they are made ; for instance, if we take the subject of roofs, shingles, slates, tin, copper, tile, felt, and composition, all have their medium pitch, or angle of inclination, that is most suited to the material : for instance, the gravel, or felt and composition covered with gravel, should always have an inclination of not more than half an inch to the foot, or the force of the water will wash away the gravel and leave bare the composition, and the felt will speedily be in a leaky condition. Slate and shingles should never be placed flatter than twenty-eight degrees of inclination ; lap shingles should have no less slope than thirty-five degrees.   Tin always looks badly when steeper than twenty-six degrees ; the same with copper, lead, and zinc, when placed upon inclined planes, but where curves are used tin looks well, wherever slate and shingles cannot be used to advantage.   Tiles should never be placed upon a roof with pitch above thirty degrees, as they would be in danger of sliding off by their own gravity.   What I have said will be sufficient to illustrate my position.   Suppose a person of mechanical mind, one balanced by practice of thought, views a building ; he sees a roof of slate or shingles, of a pitch of twenty-three or twenty-four degrees inclination ; at once his attention is arrested in the contemplation of the building. "Why," he asks himself, " is this roof so flat ? It will surely leak, the shingles rot, and the storm blow in snow and water."   All the low, leaky roofs stored in his memory will come forth, and take away from his mind much of the beauty of the building.   If it had been tin, no thoughts of the kind would intrude, but the eyes and attention would go to examining other details of the work.   Tin roofs, I have said, always look ill when placed upon steep-pitched roofs, unless a mechanical advantage in their use is obvious, as I have explained.   Slates are more lasting and durable than tin, and of as little or less cost primarily, and much less, when the successive coats of paint, which must be placed upon tin in order to make it last, are considered.   So a wise or foolish selection of materials can be made ; and the beholder viewing a structure, balances the good and bad sense of its construction in the work, and estimates its merits accordingly.

Slates may be objected to as making the rooms too warm within, therefore shingles cannot have this objection. Tin, which is generally painted red or brown, has the same objection. It has been stated to me by a friend that to whitewash the roof-boards upon the top before slating will render the rooms much cooler. We always advise and provide in our drawings for air to pass between the rafters from apertures made in the planciers, which render French roofs very comfortable, they always having false ceilings, which leave space for ventilation above.

Chimneys are very picturesque if well treated ; but one thing is necessary : as roofs should never leak, neither should chimneys ever smoke. They must be carried up above the house in order that no eddies of air blowing from any direction shall destroy their efficiency. I always send them up out of danger, and depend upon their treatment for the part they are to play in the design. All sensible persons see at a glance the necessity of their height, and approve the daring spirit that, instead of spoiling the house by smoky chimneys, does the best that can be done with the masonry thus thrown aloft.

I might go thus through the whole details of a building ; but let me for a moment dwell upon the barren geniuses who, to make their work attractive, put in false windows, empty parapets, and unnecessary appliances for the mere effect of duplication, ignorant of the fact that to duplicate ugly forms but increases the deformity. Yet certain balances in some styles are really necessary. Let your composition be such that it will be formed by an evolution of parts necessary, and part of the design.

If the few remarks I have here thrown out are duly considered, the beginner cannot fail to start in the right direction of thought to become an architect. If, however, he wishes to be merely the slavish copyist of the works of others, he can never be more than a draughtsman.

HOBBS'S RULES FOR CRITICISM.

As the whole is more important than any separate part, and equals all the parts, it demands the first and last consideration.

All architecture must be practical, and should be mechanical; and errors in this department are unbearable ignorance, and sink the architect below the artisan, who could do better.

All work, when practical and mechanical, should be beautiful, or the architect has no genius or merit.

All ugly things should be dropped as soon as possible; and all beautiful parts be made use of to the greatest extent admissible with propriety.

No part should chop up the whole unless it be worthless. There should be some master line throughout the whole work like the three colors, red, blue, and yellow, which, when balanced, produce a neutral gray or black; and so an equal balance of these three lines will produce a neutral, or as near nothing as possible.

Central ornaments, pediments, etc., must be of sufficient power to master the sides or the sides master them. If equal, the effect is neutral and the labor lost.

Make the parts which have the most important offices to perform the purest, and ornamentally attractive.

Never attract attention by ornamenting unpleasant things, as it makes them conspicuous.

Do all things with strict regard to economy.

Never use labor and material unless it pays in the design.

All false things, as string courses, false windows, chimneys, and other parts not wanted, but necessary to make a design acceptable, show lack of good architecture.

He that can use the least labor and material, and produce the most beautiful effect, is the best architect.

It is not the knowing a fact that makes men wise, but their estimation of its true value.

Learn to see the beautiful in all things; but if they have ugliness about them, never see it without condemning it.

Guard the avenues to the senses by good judgment, and let nothing foul or unsightly enter without being accompanied by an idea that will reform it; then it will lie quietly in the mind, and not come forward to disturb the good.

PREFACE.

THE majority of these designs have appeared monthly in *Godey's Ladies' Book*, from the latter part of 1863 until the present time; a few in *The Farmer*, an agricultural magazine published in Richmond, Virginia; the remainder have never before appeared in print. Induced by the flattering reception they have met with, and by constant appeals, the author has been led to offer them to the public in book form.

Original designs from the author will be continued each month in *Godey's Ladies' Book*. A noticeable feature connected with them is the fact that the greater portion of them have been executed, and, without an exception, give entire satisfaction; a more practical test of their value could not be given.

The chapters preceding the designs give practical hints in regard to the cultivation of artistic taste, choice of situation, style, construction, heating, ventilation, etc. Each design is described.

The intent of this work is not only to assist those who may be about to build, but, like the many works of the same character which have been published, to aid its readers in the cultivation of taste and the love of the beautiful, that they, too, may read "sermons in stones."

ISAAC H. HOBBS & SON, ARCHITECTS,

Office, Nos. 809 and 811 Chestnut Street.

Address to Residence, 804 North Eighth Street, Philadelphia.

DESIGN I.

THIS building was designed and built for Colonel Walter W. Price, of New York City, upon the west bank of Lake George, one and a half miles above the Fort William Henry Hotel, upon one of the most commanding situations on the lake. It is surrounded by a large plantation, which is one of the most extensive and beautiful parks in the northern part of the State of New York. Fish-ponds, groves, and all the adornments and conveniences indulged in by Europeans, are here supplied. The building is superb and grand, and its proportions are adapted to the situation.

HEIGHT OF STORIES.—First story, 14 feet in clear; second story, 13 feet; upper story, 12 feet. Cost, $35,000.

First Floor.—A, vestibule, 9 by 10 feet; B, hall, 10 feet wide; C, drawing-room, 16 feet 9 inches by 29 feet 6 inches; D, parlor, 16 feet 6 inches by 24 feet; E, sitting-room, 26 feet 9 inches by 16 feet; F, staircase-hall; G, dining-room, 22 by 17 feet 9 inches; H, breakfast-room, 17 by 18 feet; I, kitchen, 14 by 19 feet 6 inches; J, kitchen, 14 by 12 feet 6 inches; K, pantry; L, servants' stair hall; M, carriage-porch.

Second Floor.—N, dressing-room, 10 feet 9 inches by 10 feet 9 inches; O, hall, 10 feet 6 inches wide; P, principal chamber, 16 feet 6 inches by 29 feet; Q, chamber, 17 by 22 feet; R, chamber, 16 by 27 feet 6 inches; S, bath-room, 13 feet 9 inches by 9 feet; T, chamber, 18 by 18 feet; U, chamber, 15 feet 6 inches by 15 feet 6 inches; V, chamber, 16 feet 6 inches by 14 feet; W, bath-room, 4 by 8 feet.

DESIGN I.

A Model Residence.

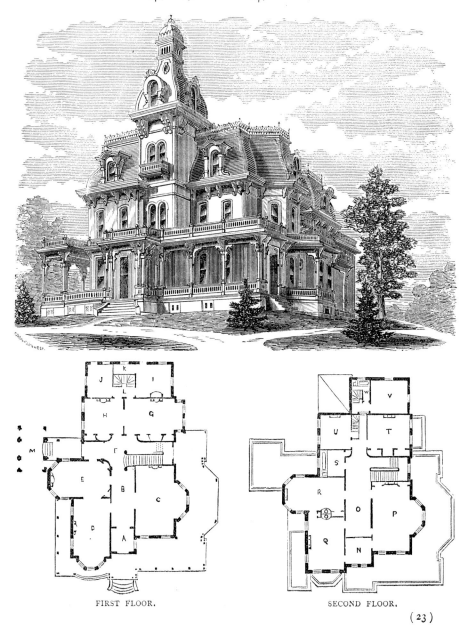

FIRST FLOOR.

SECOND FLOOR.

DESIGN II.

SUBURBAN RESIDENCE.

THIS design is a beautiful type of suburban residence, with a Mansard-roof. It was constructed in Elmira, N. Y. It was built for Mr. Reynolds, of Elmira, and its cost, when completed, was $50,000; and it will compare favorably, for internal beauty and external grandeur, with any of those princely residences built in the city of New York. It is built of brick, with Ohio sandstone finish. As will be observed, the dimensions of all its parts are upon a grand scale. The stairway is of the most superb kind. The newel-post contains a bronze figure, holding a globe. The opening of the stair above passes half-way over the hall, and the wainscoting and railing are of a carved pattern of a very grand kind. The dining-room is also extremely grand and effective, having a conservatory for flowers in the manner of a bay, with a fountain in the centre. The lower lights of glass, being made of mirrors, reflect the plants most beautifully. The floor is made of ornamental iron-work, with places between the pat-- terns for planting the flowers. The wood-work is of a new style of finish invented by ourselves.

First Floor.—A, parlor, 28 by 16 feet; B, sitting-room, 23 by 16 feet; C, library, 20 feet 10 inches by 16 feet; D, dining-room, 15 feet 9 inches by 26 feet; E, conservatory, 9 by 14 feet; F, hall, 11 by 38 feet 6 inches; G, vestibule, 8 by 11 feet; H, butler's pantry, 12 feet 6 inches by 8 feet; I, store-closet, 8 by 5 feet 3 inches; J, kitchen, 18 by 18 feet; K, nursery, 22 by 18 feet; L, lavatory, 6 by 5 feet; M, back porch; N, front porch.

DESIGN II.
Suburban Residence.

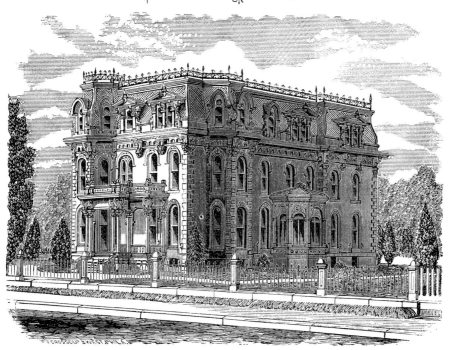

FIRST FLOOR.

DESIGN III.

SUBURBAN RESIDENCE.

THIS suburban residence is in the Italian style, with Mansard-roof and octagonal corner tower. It will have a grand effect, if built in the spirit of the design. It contains a very complete set of apartments, large and commodious, and would make an admirable riverside residence, with ample grounds, sloping gradually forward. Terrace-walks and fine finish of lawns are requisite; smooth and well-kept walks, and well-graded and closely-shaved slopes, are necessary to carry out and give full effect to the design. It has a character of rich and grand effect: nothing grotesque will be in harmony; everything must be in the highest type of refinement, vases with plants edging the walks, and the shrubbery must be grouped on the lawn in the best manner, to carry out the desired effect. It can be built for $25,000. It is intended to be built of brick, with the dressings in wood; the whole to be painted and sanded, in imitation of a warm-colored sandstone.

First Floor.—A, hall, 10 feet wide; B, reception-room, 14 by 14 feet; C, sitting-room, 14 by 21 feet; D, drawing-room, 20 by 30 feet; E, dining-room, 15 by 32 feet; F, conservatory, 16 by 25 feet; G, kitchen, 16 by 20 feet; H, servants' hall, 12 by 16 feet.

Second Floor.—L, bath- and dressing-room; M, chambers; N, billiard-room.

DESIGN III.

𝔖𝔲𝔟𝔲𝔯𝔟𝔞𝔫 𝔕𝔢𝔰𝔦𝔡𝔢𝔫𝔠𝔢.

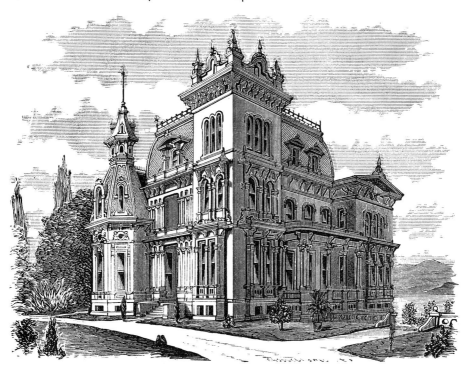

FIRST FLOOR.

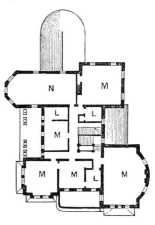

SECOND FLOOR.

DESIGN IV.

SUBURBAN RESIDENCE.

THIS design is in the Ovo order of architecture. Each detail part has its proportion, extracted without deviation or change, from the very first line to the consummation of the design. This building is designed to suit a situation upon the side of one of the ranges of the Alleghany Mountains, at Tyrone, Pa. The ground rising so rapidly demands an evolution peculiar to the situation, which is obtained by shortening the depth and increasing the length of the front. Where houses are backed by ranges of high hills, they appear very diminutive by contrast, and it is necessary to bring to our aid some stratagem by which this can be overcome. This building will be nearly one hundred and twenty-five feet front, yet have no more space in it than many first-class residences we are continually designing. The cost of the erection of this building will be about $35,000, and it is intended for the residence of Mr. Caldwell, of the firm of Caldwell & Loyd, Bankers, Tyrone.

First Floor.—A, porch; B, vestibule, 12 by 13 feet; C, library and reception-room, 13 by 16 feet; D, sitting-room, 23 feet 3 inches by 34 feet 6 inches; E, hall, 12 feet wide; F, parlor, 18 by 46 feet; G, scullery, 12 by 11 feet 6 inches; H, kitchen, 16 by 18 feet; I, stairs; J, dining-room, 16 by 33 feet; K, porch.

Height of first floor, 15 feet; second floor, 12 feet and 13 feet 6 inches; third floor, 10 feet and 12 feet 6 inches.

DESIGN IV.

Suburban Residence.

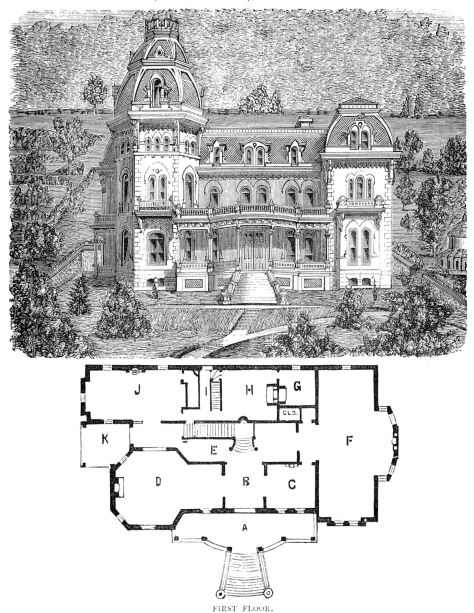

FIRST FLOOR.

DESIGN V.

SUBURBAN RESIDENCE.

THIS design, with a Mansard-roof, is intended for a town or suburban residence. It needs the association of other houses, with small plantations between, and set some sixty feet back from the road, but should always take a position on a line with others adjoining. In such a position, with well-trained grass, nicely-kept walks, with a few terra-cotta "jardinières," furnished with flowering plants, a small fountain, with a few well-chosen bushes in the rear, forming clumps impenetrable to the eye, set in such a manner as to form small vistas, but closing up the view before the rear of the lot is exposed, properly treated in this manner, a degree of refinement will be thrown over the whole that even the largest, most pretentious, or costly houses may lack. The building cost, where it is situated, on the bank of the Raritan River, at New Brunswick, N. J., $7000. It was built with the addition of a fine porch extending from bay end in the front to the left-hand side, making an improved effect. The design was made for Dr. Robbins, of the above place, and was executed to his full satisfaction.

First Floor.—A, vestibule, 4 by 6 feet; B, stair-hall, 12 by 14 feet 9 inches; C, parlor, 16 by 18 feet, with bay-window, 8 by 12 feet; D, dining-room, 14 by 16 feet, with bay-window, 4 by 9 feet; E, library, 12 by 13 feet, with bay-window, 4 by 9 feet; F, kitchen, 11 by 22 feet; G, store-room, 6 by 8 feet.

Second Floor.—Four chambers, marked M, all of sizes as rooms below; H, bath-room, 9 by 12 feet.

Third Floor contains an equal number of well-ventilated chambers; high stories.

DESIGN V.

Suburban Residence.

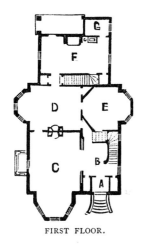

FIRST FLOOR.

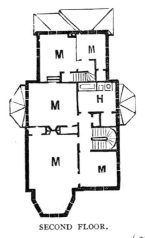

SECOND FLOOR.

DESIGN VI.

SUBURBAN RESIDENCE.

THIS design of a suburban residence contains large and ample accommodations. By reference to the plans, the rooms will be seen to be of very good proportions, and all differing in size and shape. The house is of brick, painted, with slate roof. The upper stories contain ample rooms for servants, tank- and store-room. It is finished with the base course, window dressings, corner-steps, and chimney-tops of sandstone, smoothly cut. Ample provision is made for heating, ventilation, and all modern appliances, as verandas, bays, porches, etc. The design was first made and built of frame, for Albert Dilworth, Esq., East Liberty, near Pittsburg, Pa., and is quite successful.

The sizes of rooms, etc., are marked upon the plans. The stories are 12 feet for the first; 11 feet, second story, in the clear between floors and the ceilings. Cost, $8000.

DESIGN VI.

Suburban Residence.

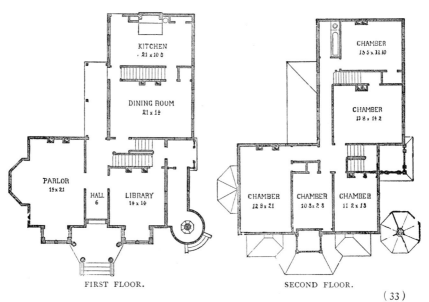

FIRST FLOOR. SECOND FLOOR.

DESIGN VII.

THIS design will make a beautiful and convenient residence, harmonizing well with a rolling country. It can be built of stone, or brick, painted; or, with some slight modifications, it can be altered to frame, if desired. It will cost about $9000.

The great beauty of such a building is in the proportion of its parts, and its adaptation to the site for its erection, whether it is to be seen at a long or short distance, as upon this a great deal will depend.

First Floor.—A, hall, 8 by 21 feet 6 inches; B, parlor, 14 feet 9 inches by 16 feet; C, library, 15 by 15 feet; D, living-room, 21 feet 5 inches by 14 feet 6 inches; E, back parlor, 14 feet 9 inches by 13 feet; F, rear hall; G, porch, 9 by 19 feet 9 inches; H, dining-room, 13 by 16 feet 3 inches; I, kitchen, 12 feet 9 inches by 13 feet 5 inches; K, porch, 13 feet 4 inches by 6 feet 8 inches.

Second Floor.—L, dressing-room; M, chamber, 14 by 15 feet; N, chamber, 15 by 13 feet 9 inches; O, chamber, 36 feet 8 inches by 14 feet 6 inches; P, chamber, 15 by 12 feet 5 inches; R, hall, 8 by 11 feet; S, chamber, 16 feet 3 inches by 13 feet; T, bathroom, 5 feet 9 inches by 8 feet 3 inches; U, bed-room, 7 feet 3 inches by 12 feet 9 inches; V, stair-hall.

DESIGN VII.
Anglo-French Villa.

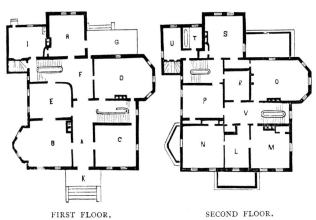

FIRST FLOOR.   SECOND FLOOR.

DESIGN VIII.

FRENCH VILLA.

THIS house is suited to the wants of a good-sized family, and furnishes liberal accommodations. The roofs are to be slated, in two tints, cut to ornamental shapes. The superstructure is to be of stone, and the verandas of wood or iron, as may be preferred. Entrance is effected through the vestibule to the main hall, which communicates with the parlor, dining-room, and stair-hall; and access to the library and kitchen is had from the rear hall.

Upon the chamber plan are five spacious chambers and the bath-room.

From the third floor a short flight of stairs leads to the tower. Cost, $8000.

First Floor.—A, vestibule, 12 by 12 feet; B, stair-hall, 12 by 12 feet; C, dining-room, 14 feet 6 inches by 29 feet 6 inches; D, kitchen, 18 by 20 feet; E, library, 18 by 20 feet; F, parlor, 20 by 28 feet 6 inches; G, main hall, 12 feet; H, rear hall, 6 feet; I, porch.

Second Floor.—K, porch-roof; L, tower-room, 12 by 12 feet; M, stair-hall; N, five chambers; O, bath-room, 12 by 12 feet; P, hall; R, back stairs.

DESIGN VIII.
French Villa.

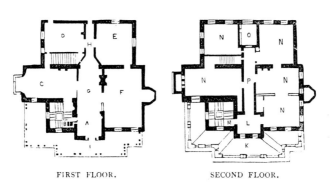

FIRST FLOOR.   SECOND FLOOR.

DESIGN IX.

ANGLO-FRENCH VILLA.

THIS design is in the Anglo-French style. In this specimen, the Grecian classic finish is harmonized, and presents to the eye the chaste elegance peculiar to Italian architecture. It will be seen at once that the building is intended to be erected of stone, with a roof of slate cut to ornamental forms. The chamber plan is arranged to meet the wants of a large family, with due regard to rooms for guests. This house would make a most desirable residence for a gentleman of means and liberal modern views. At present prices of materials and labor, it could be built in the vicinity of Philadelphia for $15,000.

The first floor contains a vestibule, two halls, a library, dining-room, drawing-room, and billiard-room. The main hall connects with the drawing-room, library, dining-room, and main staircase.

The domestic offices, such as kitchen, wash-room, etc., are placed below.

The second floor contains fine, spacious chambers, as bath-room, dressing-room, and five fine closets.

First Floor.—1, vestibule, 10 by 8 feet; 2, hall, 12 by 35 feet; 3, drawing-room, 20 by 35 feet; 4, library, 20 by 21 feet; 5, hall, 4 feet; 6, stair-hall, 10 by 14 feet; 7, 8, closets; 9, dining-room, 16 by 28 feet; 10, billiard-room, 15 by 18 feet; 11, back stair-hall, 6 by 12 feet; 12, 13, porch.

Second Floor.—14, 15, chambers, 17 by 20 feet; 16, bath-room, 8 by 10 feet; 17, chamber, 16 by 21 feet; 18, chamber, 15 by 18 feet; 19, 20, 21, closets; 22, passage, 4 feet; 23, hall; 24, closet; 25, dressing-room, 8 by 12 feet; 26, closet; 27, chamber, 20 by 21 feet; 28, 29, verandas.

DESIGN IX.

Anglo-French Villa.

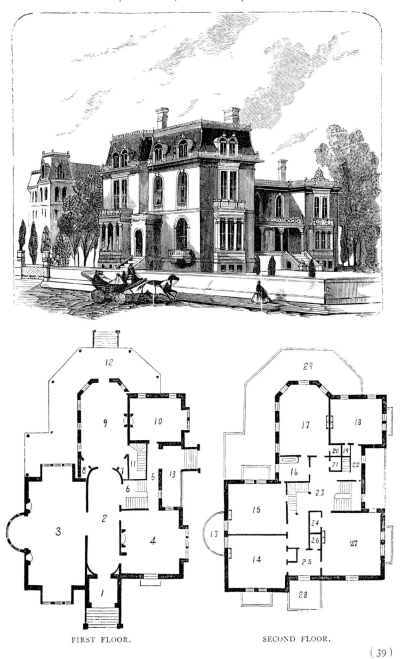

FIRST FLOOR.　　　　SECOND FLOOR.

DESIGN X.

FRENCH COUNTRY RESIDENCE.

THIS design is drawn in the French style, with American wants supplied. For a small family, it is very compact in its plan, and conveniently arranged, so that quite a stylish parlor and living-room are obtained. The kitchen is small, but when the parlor is used as a living-room, it will be found ample. This is a design which will afford real and substantial comfort to its occupants ; being small, and servants not to be had at all times, the necessity of doing your own work for a few days will not be so difficult a task. It is one that will appear larger than it really is. The interior has been carefully designed with due regard to economy of both space and expense, making it a most desirable residence for a family of moderate size.

The cost of building this house has been estimated by a builder at $2700, complete, in the vicinity of Philadelphia.

First Floor.—1, front porch, 6 by 8 feet; 2, hall, 7 feet 6 inches by 11 feet 9 inches ; 3, library, 6 feet 11 inches by 7 feet 6 inches; 4, living-room, 15 by 19 feet 1 inch ; 5, dining-room, 18 by 14 feet 2 inches ; 6, kitchen, 12 by 10 feet 2 inches ; 7, pump-shed ; 8, rear porch, on river front, 14 by 8 feet.

Second Floor.—9, hall; 10, sewing-room, 5 feet 1 inch by 5 feet 6 inches ; 11, chamber, 10 feet 9 inches by 14 feet 3 inches ; 12, chamber, 8 by 12 feet 7 inches ; 13, chamber, 14 feet 2 inches by 11 feet 3 inches ; 14, passage ; 15, bath-room, 6 feet 10 inches by 6 feet 6 inches ; 16, veranda.

DESIGN X.

French Country Residence.

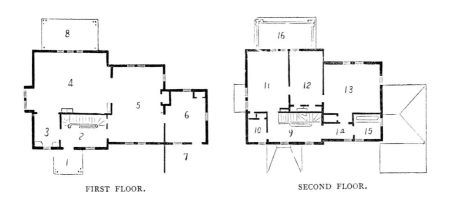

FIRST FLOOR. SECOND FLOOR.

DESIGN XI.

ROMANESQUE VILLA.

THIS villa is in the Oriental-Romanesque style, a blending of the two feelings, with the arch and dome of the Roman.

The accommodations offered by this plan are both spacious and sumptuous, making it a magnificent mansion. It should be in its surroundings assisted by fountains, statues, and other accessories, to produce the highest finished appearance.

Upon the principal floor there is a grand hall, which traverses the length of the whole building. To preclude any possibility of its having a bare appearance, the hall should be appropriately decorated with pictures. The main hall gives access to the parlor, sitting-room, ladies' retiring-room, dining-room, billiard-room, and main staircase. The dumb-waiter communicates with the kitchen. The building is intended to be erected of cut stone, or brick and stucco, with a roof of tin, ribbed.

First Floor.—1, front porch; 2, vestibule; 3, grand hall, 12 by 65 feet 6 inches; 4, sitting-room, 20 by 40 feet; 5, parlor, 20 by 40 feet; 6, alcoves; 7, stair-hall, 12 by 14 feet; 8, back stairs; 9, closet; 10, dumb-waiter; 11, ladies' retiring-room, 14 by 19 feet; 12, water-closets; 13, dining-room, 17 feet 9 inches by 28 feet 3 inches; 14, billiard-room, 17 feet 9 inches by 28 feet 3 inches; 15, side porches; 16, carriage-porch; 17, summer-house; 18, rear porch.

This plan is not necessarily an expensive one. With these dimensions it will cost, as drawn, $40,000: finely hammer-dressed stone walls; walnut finish in first and second floors; yet, by reducing the size of rooms to moderate size, stones, etc., it can be built as cheap as most other designs. The rear grounds are supposed to be lower than front, terraced down. The kitchen, laundry, etc., to be in the basement. It can be built at a range from $15,000 up.

DESIGN XI.

Romanesque Villa.

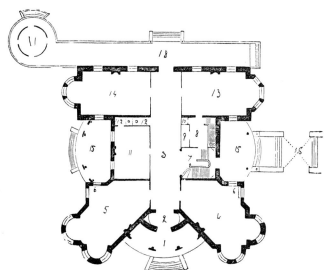

FIRST FLOOR.

DESIGN XII.

SUBURBAN RESIDENCE.

THIS design was built for Mr. Dick, Esq., of Meadville, Pennsylvania. It is built of stone, with a roof of slate; the interior has been completed in the best manner, with marble mantels, low-down grates, etc. It is sumptuous without ostentation, and an elegant home, much admired. The entire work was contracted for and finished at a cost of $40,000. The plans for the interior were designed with reference to convenience and comfort. The arrangements for heating and ventilating are admirable, and give entire satisfaction.

First Floor.—A, porch, 21 feet 6 inches by 11 feet 4 inches; B, hall, 21 feet 6 inches by 11 feet 4 inches; C, sitting-room, 17 feet 8 inches by 17 feet 10 inches; D, conservatory, 13 feet 8 inches by 10 feet 11 inches; E, chamber, 14 feet 6 inches by 14 feet 4 inches; F, bath-room, 7 feet 2 inches by 5 feet; G, water-closet; H, closet; I, dining-room, 22 feet 7 inches by 14 feet 6 inches; J, rear porch; K, waiting-hall; L, pantry, 11 feet 9 inches by 6 feet; M, kitchen, 15 feet 11 inches by 16 feet 1½ inches; N, scullery, 18 feet 10 inches by 17 feet 11 inches; O, sewing-room, 17 feet 11 inches by 10 feet; P, porch.

Second Floor.—1, veranda; 2, hall, 11 feet 3 inches; 3, library, 17 feet 8 inches by 17 feet 8 inches; 4, conservatory, 13 feet 8 inches by 10 feet 11 inches; 5, chamber, 14 feet 6 inches by 14 feet 2 inches; 6, bath-room, 6 feet 6 inches by 5 feet; 7, dressing-room, 5 by 11 feet; 8, closet; 9, chamber, 17 feet 11 inches by 14 feet 7 inches; 10, parlor, 22 feet 6 inches by 15 feet 11 inches; 11, bath-room, 11 by 9 feet 6 inches; 12, bed-room, 10 feet 11 inches by 8 feet 9 inches; 13, bed-room, 17 feet 11 inches by 10 feet; 14, 15, verandas.

Those who have seen this house pronounce it very beautiful. It is certainly a house that will arrest your attention in passing it.

DESIGN XII.

Suburban Residence.

FIRST FLOOR

SECOND FLOOR.

DESIGN XIII.

ORNAMENTAL COTTAGE.

THIS design was built by Mr. Bless, a gentleman in Newark, New Jersey, and was erected of stone, with a French roof covered with slate, cut to ornamental forms; the chimneys are finished with terra-cotta tops, thereby obtaining a light and graceful finish. The accommodations are ample, and the house is larger than one would think, at a casual glance. A plan for the laying out and embellishment of the grounds has also been designed, which harmonizes and accords well with the character of the house. It is a great success, gives full satisfaction, and cost $9000.

1, front porch; 2, hall, 7 feet 6 inches; 3, sitting-room, 15 by 20 feet; 4, parlor, 15 by 28 feet; 5, stair-hall; 6, dining-room, 15 by 20 feet; 7, china closet; 8, kitchen, 15 feet 6 inches by 16 feet 6 inches; 9, bed-room, 14 by 17 feet; 10, bath-room, 5 by 16 feet; 11, wash-house, 10 by 10 feet; 12, coal-shed, 11 feet 6 inches by 10 feet; 13, 14, side porches.

A, summer-house; B, carriage-house; C, cow-shed; D, stalls; E, harness-room; F, kitchen-garden.

While satisfactory as to beauty and compactness, yet it is situated in an unhealthy situation, with bad water, and is not at all desirable upon these points. Persons should use every care possible in selecting sites for buildings, as no architecture can compensate for the want of health in a family.

DESIGN XIII.

Ornamental Cottage.

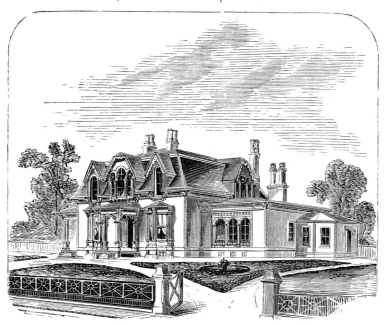

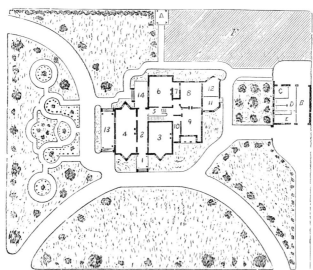

GROUND PLAN, WITH LAWN PLAT.

DESIGN XIV.

COUNTRY RESIDENCE.

THIS design was drawn as a residence for a family of moderate size. It is intended to be executed in frame, with a roof of slate. The plans are quite simple, and will explain themselves. At present range of prices it could be well built for $3000.

First Floor.—1, front porch; 2, side porch; 3, hall; 4, parlor, 13 feet 6 inches by 16 feet; 5, library, 8 feet 6 inches by 9 feet 9 inches; 6, dining-room, 13 by 17 feet; 7, 8, closets; 9, kitchen, 12 by 12 feet 6 inches; 10, porch.

Second Floor.—11, 12, verandas; 13, hall; 14, chamber, 13 by 13 feet 6 inches; 15, closet; 16, bath-room, 7 by 8 feet.

DESIGN XIV.

Country Residence

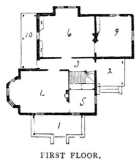

FIRST FLOOR.

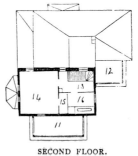

SECOND FLOOR.

DESIGN XV.

SUBURBAN RESIDENCE.

THIS design was drawn for John W. Thomas, Esq., of Chelten Hills, near Philadelphia. The work was contracted for by George Watson, Esq., builder, for a little less than $50,000, and was built of Falls of Schuylkill granite: the base being range-work, and the whole superstructure of rubble-work, pointed with white mortar, and lined by a neat black line, and all the wood-work outside painted and sanded to the color of Pictou stone. The building is considered a very beautiful one, and has a grand and imposing appearance. The details were all drawn with care and executed in a superior manner. The interior is grand, and executed chiefly in black walnut, finished without gloss.

First Floor.—1, vestibule, 7 feet 6 inches by 10 feet; 2, parlor, 17 feet 10 inches by 33 feet; 3, hall, 10 by 30 feet 10 inches; 4, sitting-room, 17 feet 10 inches by 20 feet; 5, dining-room, 17 feet 10 inches by 30 feet 10 inches; 6, servants' dining-room, 10 feet 9 inches by 18 feet 9 inches; 7, butler's pantry, 4 feet 9 inches by 6 feet 4 inches; 8, kitchen, 16 feet 3 inches by 18 feet 9 inches; 9, library, 12 by 12 feet; 10, summer kitchen, 12 by 12 feet; 11, front porch; 12, side porch.

Second Floor.—13, hall, 10 by 22 feet 10 inches; 14, dressing-room, 10 by 15 feet; 15, bath-room, 6 feet 3 inches by 8 feet 6 inches; 16, closet; 17, chamber, 11 feet 4 inches by 10 feet 9 inches; 18, chamber, 17 feet 10 inches by 20 feet; 19, chamber, 18 feet 10 inches by 15 feet 1 inch; 20, chamber, 17 feet 10 inches by 14 feet 6 inches; 21, chamber, 17 feet 10 inches by 17 feet; 22, sewing-room, 14 by 18 feet 10 inches; 23, kitchen-roof.

DESIGN XV.

Suburban Residence.

FIRST FLOOR.

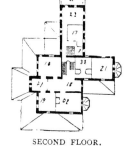

SECOND FLOOR.

DESIGN XVI.

VILLAGE OR SUBURBAN RESIDENCE.

THIS design will be very appropriate for a village or suburban residence. The interior contains all the accommodations necessary for a first-class modern residence. It will cost $8000. The superstructure will be of brick, rubbed down and painted.

The kitchen and culinary departments are placed below, and will be very well adapted, if the situation slopes to the rear.

The height of first floor is 12 feet, and second floor, 10 feet in the clear.

First Floor.—P, porch, 18 by 12 feet; L, library, 14 by 14 feet; H, hall, 8 feet; S R, sitting-room, 16 by 16 feet; D, dining-room, 15 feet 6 inches by 19 feet; D R, drawing-room, 25 by 16 feet; O P, outside porch, 10 feet.

Second Floor.—H, stair-hall, 12 feet; B R, bath-room, 16 by 16 feet; N C, nursery-chamber, 14 by 14 feet; C, chamber over porch, 16 by 18 feet; C, chamber over drawing-room, 16 by 25 feet; C, chamber over dining-room, 15 feet 6 inches by 19 feet; P R, porch-roof.

DESIGN XVI.

Village or Suburban Residence.

FIRST FLOOR.

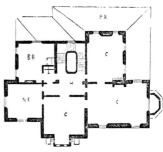

SECOND FLOOR.

DESIGN XVII.

VILLAGE OR SUBURBAN RESIDENCE.

THIS suburban or village mansion is truly American in spirit and in accommodations. It is arranged with economy, both in view of building it and in the grandeur of its interior. At a glance, the wide and long hall, or vestibule, with its elliptical staircase, must be acknowledged as a grand feature, in entering from the porch in front.

The office in the lower wing is sufficiently large for a physician, or it may be used as a boudoir. The parlor, it will be seen, is of magnificent proportions, as well as of pleasing form, capable of ceiling decorations of the most tasty kind. The piano can be placed in the bay communicating with the rear hall. It is not necessary to pass into the parlor when practicing or receiving tuition.

The dining-room will be found ample, and also beautiful, with an alcove at its end.

The kitchen apartments are conveniently placed. The establishment can be worked in first-class style with comparatively few servants. If carried out in full, it will cost $20,000. The same design can be carried out at a much less cost, if desirable.

First Floor.—1, front porch; 2, hall, 9 feet; 3, office, 13 by 13 feet; 4, parlor, 18 feet 6 inches by 34 feet; 5, sitting-room, 14 feet 6 inches by 19 feet; 6, dining-room, 15 by 25 feet; 7, kitchen, 14 feet 6 inches by 19 feet; 8, scullery, 12 by 15 feet; 9, rear porch; 10, side porch.

Second Floor.—11, hall; 12, boudoir, 13 by 13 feet; 13, bath-room, 7 by 11 feet; 14, nursery, 15 by 15 feet; 15, chamber, 22 by 19 feet; 16, chamber, 18 by 18 feet 9 inches; 17, chamber, 22 by 15 feet; 18, 19, verandas.

DESIGN XVII.

Village or Suburban Residence.

FIRST FLOOR.

SECOND FLOOR.

DESIGN XVIII.

VILLAGE OR SUBURBAN RESIDENCE.

THIS building was designed for a gentleman in the western part of this State, and has a very extensive terrace, with a pavilion, level with the porch-floor. It is drawn for stone, to be laid rubble, and pointed with dark mortar. The plan of the building is very commodious; all of the rooms, halls, etc., are large, the ceiling being thirteen feet high. The arrangement for the stairs is such that very easy ones can be built. The general character of the building is spreading and large. It cost, at the time, $20,000, and is a durable mansion, fully up to the advanced thought of the age. Buildings of the same kind vary in their cost when differently situated; the cost of materials and labor doubles in many parts, and is less in others.

First Floor.—1, front porch; 2, vestibule, 8 by 16 feet; 3, sitting-room, 16 by 33 feet; 4, parlor, 16 by 33 feet; 5, dining-room, 14 by 24 feet; 6, hall, 10 by 40 feet; 7, bed-room, 12 by 14 feet; 8, bath-room, 10 by 12 feet; 9, kitchen, 14 by 18 feet; 10, scullery, 12 by 14 feet; 11, rear porch; 12, carriage-house.

DESIGN XVIII.

Village or Suburban Residence.

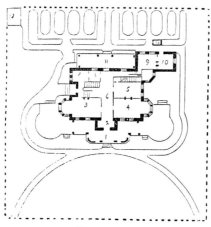

FIRST FLOOR.

DESIGN XIX.

SUBURBAN RESIDENCE.

THIS building was designed to meet the views of a gentleman residing in the suburbs of New York, and was intended to be erected on the banks of a river. To be built of stone, pointed, with a Mansard-roof, of slate.

It has all the modern appliances for a first-class residence, with fine porches, bay-windows, tower, and all the appendages requisite for an elegant home. With a good finish, it will cost $15,000.

First Floor.—1, front porch; 2, vestibule; 3, library, 20 feet 6 inches by 17 feet 5 inches; 4, parlor, 16 feet 6 inches by 39 feet 9 inches; 5, dining-room, 17 feet 3 inches by 30 feet 6 inches; 6, hall, 40 feet 6 inches by 10 feet; 7, sitting-room, 27 feet 6 inches by 16 feet 4 inches; 8, rear porch.

Second Floor.—9, chamber, 21 feet 2 inches by 16 feet 6 inches; 10, boudoir, 13 feet 4 inches by 24 feet 3 inches; 11, chamber, 21 feet 3 inches by 17 feet 3 inches; 12, chamber, 17 feet 3 inches by 19 feet 3 inches; 13, hall; 14, chamber, 21 feet 8 inches by 15 feet 4 inches; 15, bath-room, 6 feet 6 inches by 12 feet 10 inches; 16, veranda.

DESIGN XIX.

Suburban Residence.

FIRST FLOOR.

SECOND FLOOR.

DESIGN XX.

SUBURBAN RESIDENCE.

THIS building was designed for Captain Spear, of Boston, Mass. It is of a style in which pure proportion of parts is necessary. To be successful, all details must be skillfully and tastefully made. It can be built of stone, or brick tinted in light color. To paint such a building of a dark and gloomy character would be barbarous. The warmth or chilliness of the tone must be decided by the surroundings, but the intensity of color must be correct, or the design will be spoiled, in which perfection is by no means common. This design will cost $20,000.

The roof is designed for slate, cut to ornamental shapes. The verandas, cornices, etc., should be painted and sanded to correspond with the color of the superstructure.

First Floor.—1, den, 12 by 16 feet; 2, library, 16 by 16 feet; 3, porch; 4, vestibule, 9 feet 6 inches by 10 feet; 5, hall, 27 feet 6 inches by 10 feet; 6, parlor, 28 feet 6 inches by 18 feet 6 inches; 7, living-room, 21 feet by 16 feet 8 inches; 8, dining-room, 15 feet 6 inches by 23 feet 6 inches; 9, kitchen, 16 by 22 feet; 10, porch.

Second Floor.—11, 12, chambers, 14 by 16 feet; 13, 14, chambers, 18 feet 6 inches by 14 feet; 15, hall; 16, dressing-room, 13 feet 6 inches by 9 feet; 17, 18, verandas; 19, chamber, 16 feet 6 inches by 12 feet 6 inches; 20, chamber, 18 by 17 feet; 21, bath-room, 8 feet 3 inches by 9 feet; 22, bed-room, 10 feet 3 inches by 12 feet 6 inches; 23, bed-room, 11 by 16 feet.

DESIGN XX.

Suburban Residence.

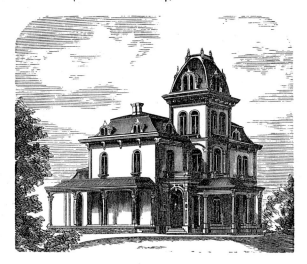

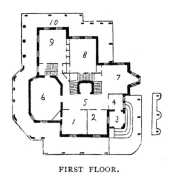

FIRST FLOOR.

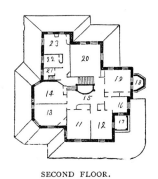

SECOND FLOOR.

DESIGN XXI.

In presenting this design of the residence of C. F. Morse, Esq., Haverhill, Mass., I do not hesitate to say that it is both beautiful and convenient. It could be built of either stone or brick, painted.

The color the building is to be painted should always be known before the same is proportioned, as the size of an object will be very different in its proportion when painted white, from that which is painted brown, or any other broken color. In fact, so many considerations must be entered into to secure a successful house, that they are rarely obtained. If successful, each part should, when viewed, appear quiet and beautiful; no part should intrude itself upon the mind so decidedly as to occupy more attention than is justly due to its office and importance, nor in any event be allowed to "chop up" the design as a whole. This is imperative, as largeness of effect and grandeur are absolutely dependent upon the principle. The cost of the house is $15,000.

First Floor.—A, portico; B, stair-hall, 15 by 17 feet; C, drawing-room, 18 by 33 feet; D, hall; E, library, 18 by 18 feet; F, winter-parlor, 16 by 21 feet; G, dining-room, 15 by 30 feet; H, breakfast-room, 16 by 18 feet; I, waiting-hall; J, porch.

Second Floor.—K, veranda; L, hall; M, chamber, 18 by 33 feet; N, chamber, 18 by 18 feet; O, chamber; P, dressing-room, 8 by 11 feet; R, chamber, 16 by 21 feet; S, back-stairs; T, chamber, 16 by 18 feet; U, bath-room, 7 by 10 feet.

DESIGN XXI.

Suburban Residence.

FIRST FLOOR.

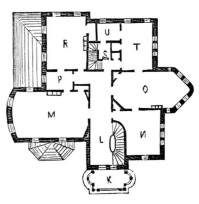

SECOND FLOOR.

(63)

DESIGN XXII.

ITALIAN VILLA.

THIS design, which is in the Italian style, was executed for Mr. D. W. C. Bidwell, Pittsburg, Pa. The greatest care has been taken with the design, both from a practical and economical point of view. There has been no unnecessary waste of room; neither was there a desire to reduce anything down to the smallest possible size. It was built of brick-hollow walls, and painted. A vestibule, carried up in the form of a tower, was thrown out in order to give additional length to the hall, and thus produce a grand effect upon entering. Three stained glass windows throw their light upon the stairway and into the hall below. A conservatory was placed over the wash-room, in connection with the nursery. The building cost $25,000, with first-quality plumbing, heating, marble mantels, etc.

First Floor.—A, vestibule, 10 by 10 feet; B, parlor, 16 by 25 feet; C, library, 22 feet 1 inch by 18 feet; D, hall, 10 feet wide; E, dining-room, 22 by 16 feet; F, lavatory, 5 by 3 feet 6 inches; G, kitchen, 19 feet 3 inches by 15 feet 6 inches; H, wash-room, 20 by 14 feet; I, pantry, 5 by 8 feet; J, china-closet, 5 by 8 feet.

Second Floor.—K, chamber, 18 feet 1 inch by 20 feet 5 inches; L, chamber, 9 feet 6 inches by 13 feet 10 inches; M, chamber, 22 by 17 feet 9 inches; N, hall, 9 feet 6 inches wide; O, chamber, 22 feet 2 inches by 16 feet 2 inches; P, bath-room, 8 feet 6 inches by 7 feet 6 inches; Q, bath-room, 8 feet 6 inches by 6 feet; R, ante-chamber, 11 feet 8 inches by 10 feet 3 inches; S, nursery, 19 feet 2 inches by 15 feet 6 inches; T, conservatory.

DESIGN XXII.

𝔍𝔱𝔞𝔩𝔦𝔞𝔫 𝔙𝔦𝔩𝔩𝔞.

FIRST FLOOR.

SECOND FLOOR.

DESIGN XXIII.

SUBURBAN VILLA.

THIS is a French-Italian suburban villa, with a Mansard-roof. It was built in New Castle, Pa., for Mr. William Patterson, a banker. Its situation is upon the side of the hill. It is of brick, painted, laid with flush joints and rubbed down. The house cost about $22,000, elegantly finished, with all the modern improvements, and is ample for a large family. The roof is of slate and tin; the porches of wood. All of the wood-work outside is sanded. The bricks are painted, but not sanded. They are of the same color as the wood-work. The sash and doors, being made of walnut, are oiled. The inside shutters are hung and made according to an invention of ours. House perfectly satisfactory.

First Floor.—A, hall, 8 feet 6 inches wide; B, parlor, 15 by 21 feet 8 inches; C, library, 16 feet 6 inches by 13 feet 9 inches; D, dining-room, 23 by 15 feet 10 inches; E, sitting-room, 18 by 12 feet 3 inches; F, kitchen, 19 by 13 feet 8 inches; G, scullery, 12 feet 5 inches by 8 feet 6 inches; H, store-room, 8 feet 6 inches by 6 feet.

Second Floor.—I, chamber, 9 feet 9 inches by 15 feet 1 inch; J, chamber, 16 feet 6 inches by 14 feet 3 inches; K, chamber, 15 feet 4 inches by 21 feet 7 inches; L, chamber, 18 feet 4 inches by 12 feet 8 inches; M, chamber, 19 feet 7 inches by 15 feet 10 inches; N, chamber, 16 feet 1 inch by 10 feet 9 inches; O, bed-room, 16 feet 1 inch by 8 feet 8 inches; P, bath-room, 6 by 8 feet.

DESIGN XXIII.

Suburban Villa.

FIRST FLOOR.

SECOND FLOOR.

DESIGN XXIV.

SUBURBAN RESIDENCE.

THIS design was drawn for Mrs. Haldeman, of Harrisburg, Pa., and the building is erected on the river-bank. It is set back from the house-line thirty feet. The parlor, dining-room, and sitting-rooms are of large proportions, and every part of the house has an air of grandeur upon entering. There is a conservatory at the rear, and an octangular bay is thrown back from it at the termination of the hall, leaving room to place a fountain.

The hall terminates with glass doors, which give a most cheerful effect to the approach to the main stairway, which is composed of walnut, with heavy double rail and carved work of ornamental design in place of balusters. The newel stands in the centre of the hall, and supports a bronze statue, forming a candelabrum. At the landing, directly in front of the hall, is a circular window of ornamental stained glass, throwing a varied tint over the stairway and entrance.

It cost $23,000, but has the appearance of and would sell for more than hundreds that are built, costing over $50,000.

First Floor.—A, vestibule, 6 feet 6 inches by 10 feet; B, hall, 10 feet wide; C, parlor, 17 by 43 feet; D, sitting-room, 16 by 20 feet 6 inches; E, back-stairway; F, dining-room, 16 by 23 feet; G, dumb-waiter; H, china closet; I, conservatory.

Second Floor.—K, sitting-room; L, alcove; M, chambers; N, bath-room; O, closets; P, hall; R, balcony.

Height of first floor from pavement, 5 feet; first story in clear, 14 feet; second, 13 feet; third, 13 feet.

DESIGN XXIV.

Suburban Residence.

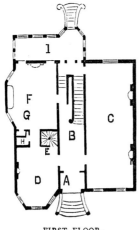

FIRST FLOOR.

SECOND FLOOR.

DESIGN XXV.

MODEL RESIDENCE.

This representation of a twin dwelling, as built for Mr. H. S. Bollman, of Pittsburg, Pa., clearly demonstrates to what an extent the architecture of this country could be improved by this mode of building.

Instead of erecting small and insignificant-looking houses, and scattering them around here and there, without adaptability of location, why not, by some mutual arrangement, let parties work together, and, selecting some pretty and convenient site, there erect a building an ornament to the neighborhood? By this mode you can secure better accommodations inside, and tenfold the beauty of exterior effect, with much less expense than by building separately. The rooms are all large and well lighted, with all the modern conveniences, — bay-windows, bath-rooms, etc. The third story can contain three chambers, with all necessary closet room, etc. The building, as here represented, is intended for stone, but could readily be altered to either brick or wood. It would cost, of stone, between $9000 and $10,000.

First Floor.—A, parlors, 16 feet 6 inches by 18 feet; B, halls; C, sitting-rooms, 14 feet 3 inches by 10 feet; D, dining-rooms, 21 feet 6 inches by 12 feet; E, kitchens, 14 feet 3 inches by 14 feet; F, sculleries, 10 by 13 feet; G, porches.

Second Floor.—H, chambers; I, bath-rooms; J, closets; K, balconies.

DESIGN XXV.

Model Residence.

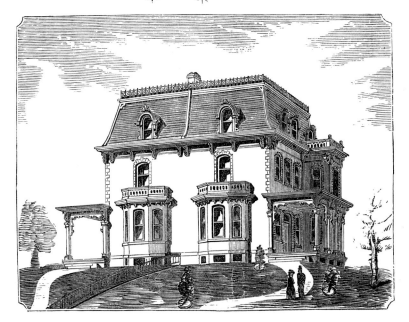

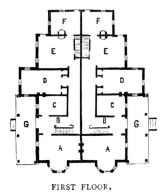

FIRST FLOOR.

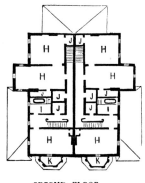

SECOND FLOOR.

DESIGN XXVI.

SUBURBAN RESIDENCE.

THIS design was built by Mr. C. S. Kauffman, of Columbia, Pa. He had the building nearly completed, when it was burned down, but rebuilt by the same plans, without alteration, showing clearly that it was fully satisfactory to the owner. We can further say, that no case has yet occurred where, when our designs have been burnt, that the building has not been reproduced upon the same plan, unaltered.

Ground Plan.—A, front porch; B, vestibule, 8 by 8 feet; C, hall, 8 feet wide; D, parlor, 16 by 31 feet; E, sitting-room, 16 by 18 feet; F, library, 15 by 28 feet; G, dining-room, 14 by 29 feet; H, kitchen, 16 by 20 feet; I, pantry; K, wash-room, 12 by 14 feet; L, porches; M, balconies.

DESIGN XXVI.

Suburban Residence.

GROUND PLAN.

DESIGN XXVII.

A MODEL RESIDENCE.

This design is a one-story and French-roof building, suitable for the Southern country. It is provided with sufficient height to admit of an air-space between the roof and second story. The design can be built in wood for about $3000, and be very comfortable and convenient. All of these designs are beautiful, because they are well-proportioned, and not merely on account of the style or order of architecture to which they belong.

We have made several modifications of this design for California, Nevada, Colorado, and other points in the United States; and they have proved satisfactory with all. Of a necessity, their proportions are all altered somewhat to suit situations; also to meet the wants of the family in regard to sizes of rooms, extent of porches, closets, etc. Hardly two persons want exactly the same house—perfectly similar inside and outside. The grounds and portions of view are apt to be different; one may face north, others south, etc., and demand different attention.

First Floor.—A, hall, 8 feet wide; B, parlor, 18 by 20 feet; C, library, 14 by 16 feet; D, dining-room, 14 by 16 feet; E, chamber, 12 by 14 feet; F, kitchen, 16 by 17 feet; G, china-closet; H, porch.

Second Floor.—K, chambers; L, bath-room; M, veranda.

DESIGN XXVII.

A Model Residence.

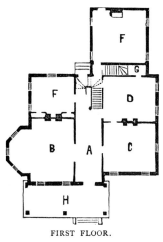

FIRST FLOOR.

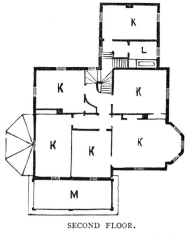

SECOND FLOOR.

DESIGN XXVIII.

SUBURBAN RESIDENCE.

THIS design was built for Mr. J. McCormick, and is situated upon the corner of Locust Street and the river-bank, in the city of Harrisburg, and is considered a successful building for proportion and grand appearance. It maintains a solid, mansion-like effect. The windows are large, ceilings lofty, and the material, cut limestone, laid broken range and pointed. The cost, finished, was about $20,000. Some considerable beauty rests in the material, which, with good architecture, should always be left so that it strikes the beholder with full force. We have invented a new order of architecture, "The American-Ovo order of architecture," for church buildings and large public edifices. It is far superior to the most elaborate styles of the highest type of flowered Gothic or Mediæval architecture.

First Floor.—A, porch; B, hall, 9 feet wide; C, parlor, 17 by 30 feet; D, sitting-room, 15 by 16 feet; E, library, 15 by 18 feet; F, dining-room, 17 feet 6 inches by 22 feet; G, kitchen, 16 by 18 feet; H, china-closet; J, pantry; K, porch.

Second Floor.—L, chamber, 17 by 22 feet; M, chamber, 19 by 17 feet 4 inches; N, chamber, 16 feet 3 inches by 15 feet; O, chamber, 17 feet 8 inches by 16 feet 9 inches; P, chamber, 14 feet 9 inches by 18 feet; R, chamber, 14 by 18 feet; S, bath-room.

DESIGN XXVIII.

Suburban Residence.

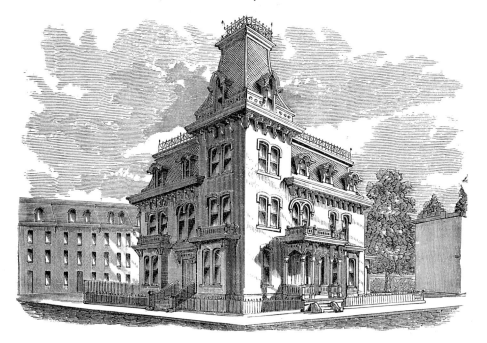

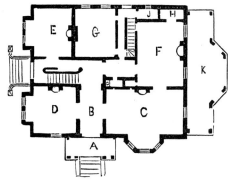

FIRST FLOOR.

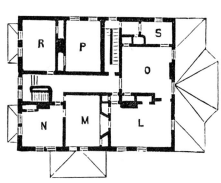

SECOND FLOOR.

(77)

DESIGN XXIX.

A MODEL RESIDENCE.

THIS residence is being built for Mr. John Bowers, of New Castle, Pa. It contains many interesting features, and was prepared for an elevated position. The roof is of the Mansard pattern, adjusted perspectively to the elevation of the site. Great economy has been used in the design, and the whole building is ornamental. Its plain surfaces are made to give to the beholder great beauty, every size having been strictly calculated by the Ovo law of architectural proportion. The musical ratios are perfectly adhered to, varied by perspective position, which pleases those beholding the structure.

The building is being built of brick, and painted, and will cost, nicely finished, about $8000, with all modern conveniences.

First Floor.—A, vestibule, 7 feet 6 inches by 6 feet; B, hall, 7 feet 6 inches wide; C, parlor, 23 feet 6 inches by 18 feet; D, library, 15 by 21 feet; E, sitting-room, 15 by 15 feet; F, dining-room, 14 by 23 feet 9 inches; G, kitchen, 14 by 15 feet 9 inches; H, pantry under stairway; I, china-closet; K, porch.

Second Floor.—L, chamber, 9 feet 3 inches by 12 feet; M, chamber, 17 by 23 feet 6 inches; N, chamber, 15 by 21 feet; O, chamber, 15 by 15 feet; P, bath-room, 5 by 8 feet; Q, chamber, 14 by 23 feet 9 inches; R, servants'-room, 12 feet 9 inches by 8 feet 9 inches; S, hall; T, store-closet; U, balcony.

(78)

DESIGN XXIX.

A Model Residence.

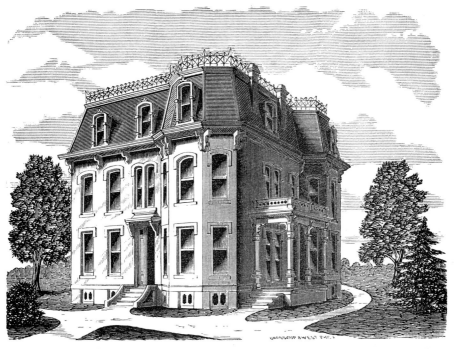

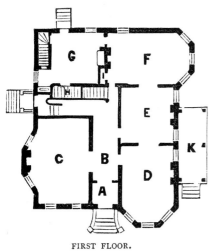

FIRST FLOOR.

SECOND FLOOR.

(79)

DESIGN XXX.

SUBURBAN OR RIVER-SIDE RESIDENCE.

THE plan of this residence was carefully prepared for economy and airy effect, and the same care has been taken to give it the appearance of being quite commodious. The cost of its erection will not exceed $4000, with all the modern improvements, such as heater, water, etc. This plan is peculiarly adapted to a situation where the ground rises rapidly behind the house, or upon the slope of a hill.

First Floor.—A, parlor, 11 feet 9 inches by 19 feet 6 inches; B, sitting-room, 12 feet 6 inches by 12 feet 9 inches; C, dining-room, 20 feet 3 inches by 13 feet 3 inches; D, kitchen, 8 feet 3 inches by 13 feet 3 inches; E, pantry, 6 feet 3 inches by 8 feet 3 inches.

Second Floor.—C, chambers, 11 feet 9 inches by 19 feet 6 inches; 12 feet 6 inches by 12 feet 9 inches; 20 feet 3 inches by 13 feet 3 inches; D, bath-room, 8 feet 3 inches by 9 feet; E, closets.

DESIGN XXX.

Suburban or River-side Residence.

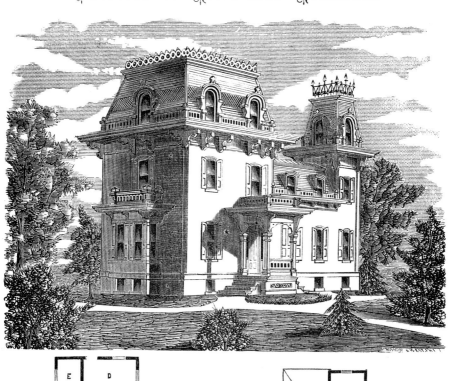

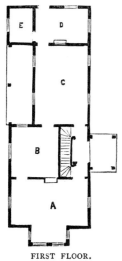

FIRST FLOOR.

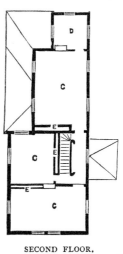

SECOND FLOOR.

DESIGN XXXI.

ORNAMENTAL FRENCH VILLA.

THIS villa is intended to be constructed of rubble-pointed masonry. The building is quite commodious, and of strictly suburban design. The plans are well arranged, and allow large and free apartments. The roof should have ornamental slates upon it. The porch is wide, and the roof projects considerably beyond the columns. It is drawn in simple elevation, but when viewed in perspective would have a much better effect.

The stories are as follows: first story, 11 feet; second, 10 feet; third, 9 feet; fourth, 9 feet. The building will cost about $10,000, and be placed 48 feet back from the street.

First Floor.—A, vestibule, 9 by 9 feet; B, sitting-room, 16 by 32 feet; C, parlor, 16 by 32 feet; D, drawing-room, 16 by 24 feet; E, dining-room, 16 by 24 feet; F, kitchen, 18 by 20 feet; G, hall, 9 by 39 feet; H, porches.

The vestibule is made to communicate with main and rear halls.

Second Floor.—I, roofs of porches and bay-windows; K, chambers: those over parlor and sitting-room, 16 by 26 feet, and those over drawing-room and dining-room, 16 by 24 feet; L, dressing-room, 9 by 15 feet.

DESIGN XXXI.

Ornamental French Villa.

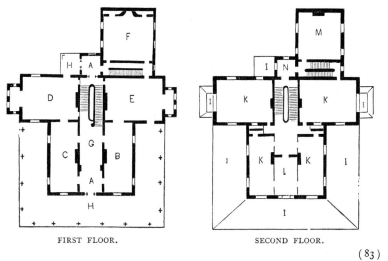

FIRST FLOOR.　　　　SECOND FLOOR.

DESIGN XXXII.

SUBURBAN RESIDENCE.

This design is in the Gothic style. It is well-adapted for a parsonage, and makes a very airy house. Built in a proper situation, it will present a good effect, and add beauty to the scenery. The above was built of frame weather-boards, nicely finished inside, at a cost of about $7000. It contains inside shutters, and all the modern conveniences.

We have recently received a patent for a new mode of hanging "pivot blinds," doing away with the bar that moves the slats by the substitution of a small brass rod that runs up the stiles. The whole is moved by a lever upon a master slat. They look very beautiful, and are free to look through, and can be cleaned as easily as tight shutters. When properly made, they close so tight that all air and dust are excluded.

First Floor.—A, main hall, 9 feet wide; B, parlor, 15 by 20 feet; C, sitting-room, 13 by 21 feet; D, dining-room, 14 by 14 feet; E, kitchen, 11 by 14 feet; F, front porch.

Second Floor.—G, study, 9 by 12 feet; H, chambers; I, bath-room, 7 by 8 feet.

DESIGN XXXII.

Suburban Residence.

FIRST FLOOR.

SECOND FLOOR.

(85)

DESIGN XXXIII.

ENGLISH-GOTHIC RESIDENCE.

THIS design is in the style of English-Gothic, drawn in the proportions of the Ovo order, which gives it a degree of refinement that suits the ideas of the American people. The principal floor contains a fine parlor, dining-room, sitting-room, kitchen, stair-hall, and vestibule, with one inclosed hall under the tower. There is a rear porch or veranda, entered from the hall by a door, and by windows reaching to the floor on the parlor. The second floor has four fine apartments, lighted by dormer- and gable-windows. The cost of the building, erected in the spirit of the design, will be $6500.

First Floor.—A, vestibule; B, inclosed hall, 8 by 8 feet; C, stair-hall, 8 feet wide; D, parlor, 15 by 25 feet; E, sitting-room, 12 feet 6 inches by 12 feet 6 inches; F, dining-room, 12 feet 6 inches by 20 feet; G, kitchen, 12 feet 6 inches by 12 feet 6 inches; H, porch.

Second Floor.—I, bed-room, 15 by 25 feet; J, stair-hall; K, bath-room; L, bed-room, 12 feet 6 inches by 12 feet 6 inches; M, bed-room, 12 feet 6 inches by 20 feet; N, bed-room, 12 feet 6 inches by 12 feet 6 inches.

DESIGN XXXIII.

English-Gothic Residence.

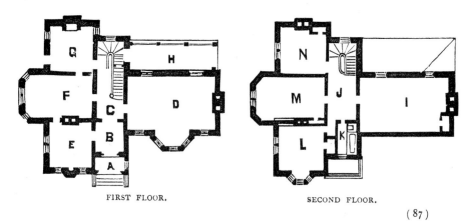

FIRST FLOOR.

SECOND FLOOR.

DESIGN XXXIV.

SMALL COTTAGE.

THIS is a design for a small cottage. It is plain and simple in construction, and is suitable for a gardener's cottage or a gate-house to a mansion, and will also make a very beautiful house for a mechanic. It is situated a short distance from the road, with a garden in front. It can be erected of frame for about $1200. The cottage will make a very beautiful home for a small family, and, with well-trimmed shrubbery, will be very attractive. It can also be built of plank, which will make it very warm and durable, and cost less.

First Floor.—A, parlor, 12 by 18 feet; B, porch, 9 feet 6 inches by 14 feet; C, hall; D, dining-room, 10 by 14 feet; E, chamber, 10 by 13 feet 6 inches; F, kitchen, 10 feet 6 inches by 12 feet; G, china-closet; I, closets.

The second story contains three chambers, H, with closets, stairs, hall, etc.

DESIGN XXXIV.

𝔖𝔪𝔞𝔩𝔩 𝔠𝔬𝔱𝔱𝔞𝔤𝔢.

FIRST FLOOR.

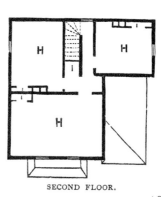

SECOND FLOOR.

(89)

DESIGN XXXV.

A SMALL COTTAGE.

THIS design is for a cheap small cottage. It can be built for about $1500, and, in some secluded situation, it would be very appropriate and beautiful. The plans themselves explain the size of the rooms.

Cheap cottages are seldom built from architects' designs and drawings, which, I think, is a great error. Why should we not have beautiful designs for the small as well as the large? The time is surely coming when the persons desiring fine homes will build their dwellings from more matured designs than they do at the present day. To have them beautiful, convenient, and adapted to situations, costs no more than abortions of taste, many of which are miserable copies of sometimes good, but ofttimes of deformed, originals.

First Floor.—A, living-room, 10 by 14 feet; B, porch, 6 feet 6 inches; C, hall, 9 feet 6 inches by 5 feet 6 inches; D, kitchen, 10 by 12 feet.

Second Floor.—H, principal chamber, 10 by 14 feet; I, hall, 9 feet 6 inches by 5 feet 6 inches; P, P, chambers, 10 by 7 feet.

DESIGN XXXV.

A Small Cottage.

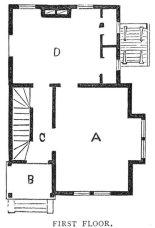

FIRST FLOOR.

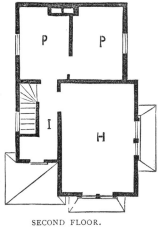

SECOND FLOOR.

DESIGN XXXVI.

SUBURBAN RESIDENCE.

This design is in the decorated suburban style, and, when carried out in detail, will form a very desirable residence: one possessing fine accommodations and comfort, with great economy of internal arrangement. It will be found, by a close examination of the plans, that all the working parts of the house are private, commodious, and convenient. It is capable of being an ornament to any locality if the proportions of its parts are properly balanced, and the building made to harmonize with its surroundings. This can only be done by those who have the true key to proportion and adaptation. Cost, $10,000. Superstructure is of bricks, painted, with all the improvements, water, gas, etc.

First Floor.—A, parlor, 16 by 23 feet; B, sitting-room, 16 by 15 feet 8 inches; C, dining-room, 19 feet 6 inches by 15 feet; D, kitchen, 14 by 18 feet; E, wash-room, 11 feet 4 inches by 11 feet 6 inches; F, pantry, 4 by 6 feet; G, lavatory, 4 by 4 feet; H, hall, 10 feet wide; 1, front porch; 2, side porch; 3, rear porch.

Second Floor.—I, chamber, 14 feet 5 inches by 23 feet; J, hall, 10 feet wide; K, dressing-room, 8 by 12 feet; L, chamber, 16 feet 5 inches square; M, chamber, 19 feet 4 inches by 14 feet 10 inches; N, bath-room, 6 by 7 feet; O, lavatory, 4 feet 6 inches by 3 feet 10 inches; P, chamber, 17 feet 8 inches by 13 feet 10 inches; Q, chamber, 14 feet 6 inches by 14 feet 11 inches; 4, 5, 6, 7, 8, verandas.

DESIGN XXXVI.

Suburban Residence.

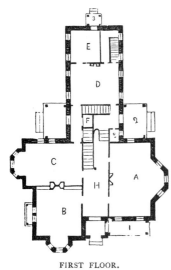

FIRST FLOOR.

SECOND FLOOR.

(93)

DESIGN XXXVII.

COTTAGE IN THE POINTED STYLE.

THIS cottage was designed for a gentleman in Salem, Ill. The superstructure is of brick, and the roof of slate, cut in ornamental shapes. It contains ample accommodations for a small family, and possesses conveniences, such as bath-room, water-closet, low-down grates, etc. The exterior is very pleasing, and is capable of a much higher degree of ornamentation than is shown in the engraving. The house can be built for $5000. It can be modified to preserve the external appearance; yet, by leaving out such conveniences as bath-room, etc., which can be added to the house at any time in the future, it can be built for $3000, if built of frame.

First Floor.—A, hall; B, sitting-room, 16 by 16 feet; C, parlor, 16 by 20 feet; D, dining-room, 13 feet 11 inches by 20 feet; E, kitchen, 13 feet 11 inches by 12 feet; F, scullery, 8 feet 5 inches by 6 feet 4 inches; G, china-closet; H, sewing-room, 10 by 6 feet 4 inches.

Second Floor.—I, bath-room, 5 feet 2 inches by 8 feet; J, bed-room, 8 feet 6 inches by 10 feet; K, chamber, 13 feet 4 inches by 15 feet 2 inches; L, chamber, 13 feet 4 inches by 12 feet; M, chamber, 13 feet 8 inches by 15 feet 11 inches; N, chamber, 18 feet 9 inches by 15 feet; O, hall; P, balcony.

DESIGN XXXVII.

Cottage in the Pointed Style.

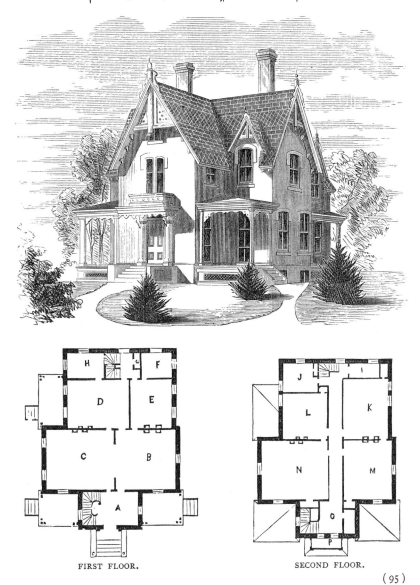

FIRST FLOOR.   SECOND FLOOR.

DESIGN XXXVIII.

SUBURBAN RESIDENCE.

THIS design was erected for A. A. Carrier, Esq., Bellfield, three miles above Pittsburg. It is beautifully situated, removed from the smoke of the city, and only a few minutes' drive from it. It is surrounded with ample grounds, and finished in the most workmanlike manner. It cost about $14,000, and is now finished; and we are enabled to say, without hesitation, that there are few that are superior in the country as to external beauty or internal comfort. We have seven dwellings and one church within view of this building, which makes it one of the most attractive spots about Pittsburg. They are all varied in design, no two of them being alike, yet a thread of harmony runs through them, and, when viewed separately, a something is seen in each peculiar only to itself.

First Floor.—1, vestibule; 2, hall, 9 feet; 3, parlor, $17\frac{1}{2}$ by 22 feet; 4, sitting-room, 15 by 18 feet; 5, dining-room, $17\frac{1}{2}$ by 20 feet; 6, library, 14 by $19\frac{1}{2}$ feet; 7, kitchen, $15\frac{1}{2}$ by 19 feet; 8, scullery, 14 by 19 feet; porches, 6 by 9 feet.

Second Floor.—10, principal chamber, $17\frac{1}{2}$ by 22 feet; 11, chamber, 15 by 18 feet; 12, chamber, $17\frac{1}{2}$ by 20 feet; 13, bell-room, 14 by $15\frac{1}{2}$ feet; 14, bell-room, 14 by 19 feet; 15, dressing-room, 14 by 15 feet; 16, hall, 9 feet; 17, 19, verandas.

DESIGN XXXVIII.

Suburban Residence.

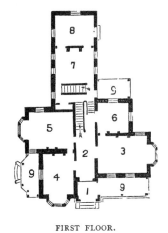

FIRST FLOOR.

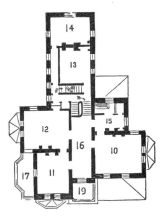

SECOND FLOOR.

(97)

DESIGN XXXIX.

PICTURESQUE VILLA.

THIS picturesque villa was erected at Bellfield, near Pittsburg, for S. S. Carrier, Esq., and is universally admired for its beauty. It stands back from the road nearly one hundred feet. The road bends a little in its approach to the house, which brings its sides into full view. It stands upon a slight elevation of about a half-inch to a foot, which is a very good grade. The roof is very fine. It turns up, like Chinese roofs, at the eaves, which gives to it an exceedingly graceful appearance. Being elaborately and beautifully finished, its cost is $14,000; but its appearance would lead one to expect it cost upwards of $40,000. Great care has been taken with its proportions, as well as with the convenience of its plans, as will be apparent upon examination.

First Floor.—A, vestibule; B, sitting-room, 16 by 15 feet 8 inches; C, parlor, 16 by 23 feet; D, dining-room, 19 feet 6 inches by 13 feet; E, kitchen, 18 by 14 feet; F, scullery, 11 feet 5 inches by 11 feet 6 inches; H, porches; I, K, L, closets.

Second Floor.—M, chamber, 16 feet 5 inches square; N, chamber, 14 feet 5 inches by 23 feet; O, chamber, 19 feet 4 inches by 14 feet 10 inches; P, another chamber; Q, chamber, 11 feet 6 inches by 14 feet 11 inches; R, balcony; S, dressing-room, 8 feet 8 inches by 12 feet; T, hall; U, closets.

DESIGN XXXIX.

Picturesque Villa.

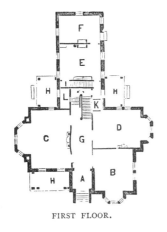

FIRST FLOOR.

SECOND FLOOR.

DESIGN XL.

SUBURBAN RESIDENCE.

THIS design is a plain and ordinary kind of building, simply having those necessary parts common to all houses, with a porch, bay-, and projecting window, with a hood projecting over a twin window in the front. The plan is so arranged as to give it the appearance of largeness. People who are not versed in the true principle of design think every part should be of equal beauty. If so, the design would be meagre. Some feature must be predominant and strong, and something must be weak, or such a result cannot be obtained. This house, built of frame, in very good style, will cost between $3000 and $4000, with marble mantels, heaters, bath, and closets. We have had many orders for full drawings and specifications, etc., for this house. They have all proved satisfactory. In some localities they cost much more than we here state—some as high as $8000, others at prices stated. All depends upon the elaborate work desired and the cost of materials constructed with.

First Floor.—A, hall, 6 feet wide ; B, parlor, 15 by 23 feet 9 inches ; C, sitting-room, 13 by 13 feet ; D, dining-room, 15 by 21 feet ; E, kitchen, 13 by 11 feet 9 inches ; F, G, porches.

Second Floor.—H, chamber, 15 by 23 feet 9 inches ; I, chamber, 13 by 13 feet ; J, chamber, 15 by 21 feet ; K, chamber, 13 by 14 feet 9 inches ; L, hall, 6 feet wide.

DESIGN XL.

Suburban Residence.

FIRST FLOOR.

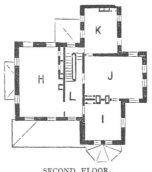

SECOND FLOOR.

DESIGN XLI.

ORNAMENTAL COTTAGE.

THIS cottage was designed and built for Mr. E. S. Mayes, of Lebanon, Ky. The plan is arranged for comfort and convenience, and its form produces a beautiful variety in the outlines of the building. It will also be noticed that no waste room occurs. The three principal rooms—sitting-, dining-room, and parlor—open directly into the front hall, which, being of large dimensions and of a room-like shape, denotes an amplitude of space on entering. There is also a beautiful staircase on one side of it. Attached to the kitchen, there is a large store-room and pantry. The second story contains four large chambers, each having a fireplace and clothes-press in them. They are all free and private. The house being of a compact and convenient form, great economy of construction is obtained. No back stairs were desired by this party, but such can easily be placed between the dining-room and the kitchen. It is constructed of bricks, laid with flush joints, and painted, as the red color of the bricks would too severely contrast with foliage. This building will cost between $4000 and $5000, with bath, tank, hot and cold water, and heater.

Description.—A, front porch; B, hall, 12 by 18 feet; C, parlor, 16 by 20 feet 7 inches; D, sitting-room, 13 feet 10 inches by 19 feet; E, dining-room, 18 by 18 feet; F, kitchen, 16 by 18 feet; G, store-room, 9 by 9 feet; H, side porch.

DESIGN XLI.

Ornamental Cottage.

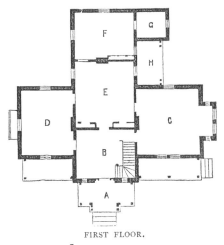

FIRST FLOOR.

DESIGN XLII.

SUBURBAN RESIDENCE.

THIS ornamental suburban residence was designed for Mrs. Fahnstock, who was about building it when she died, and the work was abandoned. Since we have published it in "Godey's Ladies' Book," the design has met with much favor, and we have made numerous evolutions of the same idea, arranged, of course, in each case to meet the wants of the parties ordering the drawings. It is always best for us to make the full detail drawings for these designs, as our experience with them is very great. There is no risk of ugliness when we make the detail drawings for our designs, as almost every locality over this vast country fully proves; and the amount of patronage we receive fully attests their merits. It can be built for $7000.

Description.—A, vestibule; B, hall, 8 feet wide; C, parlor, 14 by 22 feet; D, dining-room, 14 by 20 feet; E, sitting-room, 14 by 16 feet; F, china-closet, 7 by 10 feet; G, pantry, 7 by 10 feet; H, kitchen, 14 by 14 feet; I, back porch; J, wash-house, 10 feet 6 inches by 10 feet 5 inches.

DESIGN XLII.

Suburban Residence.

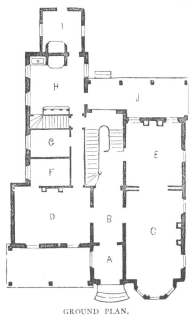

GROUND PLAN.

DESIGN XLIII.

SUBURBAN RESIDENCE.

THIS beautiful cottage was designed and built for Mr. Wm. Jackson, near Pittsburg, Pa., and is a very commodious and comfortable residence. It is built on the slope of a hill, and entirely surrounded by large forest-trees. Its peculiar plan affords the greatest possible capacity, as the hall, dining-room, sitting-room, and parlor can be thrown into one grand room, which, being connected with back and front porches by windows running to the floor, contains a very large area, so that thirty sets of cotillions have danced at one time. The kitchen apartments are entirely separate. It has been occupied for four years, and the owner has remarked that if he were to build another house he would not alter, in a single particular, any portion of it. The house cost the owner $15,000, but we will place it by the side of many costing $30,000, for capacity and grand interior, as well as largeness of external appearance.

First Floor.—A, stair hall, 16 by 22 feet; B, parlor, 18 by 30 feet; C, sitting-room, 16 by 22 feet; D, dining-room, 18 by 18 feet; E, kitchen, 13 by 18 feet; F, scullery, 6 by 10 feet 6 inches; G, pantry, 6 by 7 feet; H, porches.

Second Floor.—K, chambers; L, bath-room; M, linen-closet.

DESIGN XLIII.

Suburban Residence.

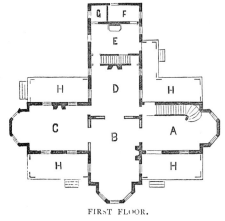

FIRST FLOOR.

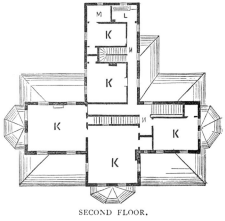

SECOND FLOOR.

DESIGN XLIV.

ORNAMENTAL COTTAGE.

BEFORE us is a cheap and ornamental cottage, of small pretensions as to classical style, but of a class largely built by those wishing the comforts of a home upon a small capital. The cost of its erection will not exceed $1500. It contains three rooms, parlor, dining-room, and kitchen, on the first floor, and three chambers on the second. The roof is so constructed as to admit of the circulation of air between the cornice and the roof as high as the ceiling: the upper part above the ceiling-joists, or collar-beam, affording a sufficient air-chamber, with a ventilator at each gable; one going down to within a few inches of the collar-beams, and passing but a small distance above the roof; the other being several feet higher, and terminating immediately below the roof, will act as a constant ventilator, owing to the difference in the pressure of the air, and render the upper stories very pleasant.

First Floor.—1, vestibule, 3½ feet wide by 4½ feet long; 2, back porch, 8 feet wide by 15 feet long; 3, living-room, 12 by 18 feet in clear; 4, kitchen, 15 by 18 feet; 5, parlor, 12 by 18 feet; 6, a small entry, affording entrance to the living-room and parlor, and the stairway leading to the cellar, which should be under the front wing.

In the second floor the rooms are private, and all entered from the passage at the top of the stairs. No waste room occurs in this plan; therefore it is cheap and convenient.

It was designed to be built of frame, with shingle roof.

DESIGN XLIV.

Ornamental Cottage.

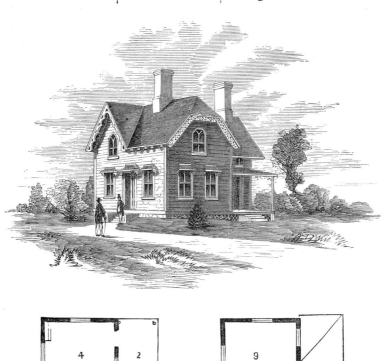

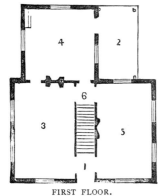

FIRST FLOOR.

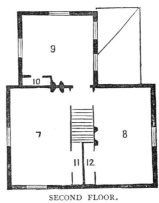

SECOND FLOOR.

DESIGN XLV.

MODEL RESIDENCE.

THIS building was designed for Charles Towne, Esq., Moorestown, N. J. He had been reading Mrs. Stowe's admirable work on "House Economy," and had taken advantage of many of her valuable suggestions that aid materially in the adjustment of the various parts, although they were intended by the author for cheapness.

This cottage is very beautiful in the exterior, and handy in the interior arrangement. By reference to the plans, it will be observed that the house is commodious, and contains everything usual in good buildings. The whole cost, when finished, $7000, built of frame. Its beauty will depend upon its proportion. All of the various parts can only be shown upon the drawings, where full details are made. More than two-thirds of buildings being built, and having a cheap, commonplace appearance, is in not supplying the builders with full and matured details of different parts, although the small scale drawings were gotten up by a good and competent architect.

First Floor.—A, entrance porch; B, hall, 9 feet wide; C, parlor, 13 by 18 feet 6 inches; D, sitting-room, 13 by 18 feet 6 inches; E, dining-room, 14 feet 3 inches by 18 feet; F, kitchen, 12 by 13 feet 6 inches; G, china-closet, 3 feet 6 inches by 6 feet; H, retiring-room, 7 by 10 feet; J, porches; K, stair-hall.

Second Floor.—M, chambers; N, servants' room; O, bath-room; P, hall; R, veranda; S, alcove.

DESIGN XLV.

Model Residence.

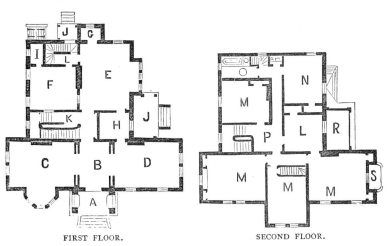

FIRST FLOOR.

SECOND FLOOR.

DESIGN XLVI.

SUBURBAN RESIDENCE.

THIS design was drawn for Mr. S. G. Coffin, Alleghany City, and was built at Edgewater, on the Alleghany Valley Railroad. The building was designed to suit a sloping situation, upon the side of a high hill. It has given great satisfaction, and those who have seen it think it the finest in the vicinity. It cost, complete, $9000.

The inner accommodations can be seen by the plans; being convenient, commodious, and admirably adapted to the position.

First Floor.—A, vestibule, 5 by 8 feet; B, hall, 8 feet wide; C, parlor, 12 by 24 feet; D, sitting-room, 14 by 14 feet; E, kitchen, 12 by 14 feet; F, dining-room, 14 by 18 feet; G, porches.

Second Floor.—H, stair-hall; I, bath-room; K, chambers.

This building has given great satisfaction, and has resulted in orders for two other buildings within sight of this, which are now being erected.

DESIGN XLVI.

Suburban Residence.

FIRST FLOOR.

SECOND FLOOR.

(113)

DESIGN XLVII.

MODEL RESIDENCE.

THIS design is a good specimen of architecture, in the pointed American style of house architecture. The plan is convenient and commodious, and can be built for about $7000. The general effect of this building is of a lofty character,—having the vertical line predominating throughout. It will be beautiful if placed in a grove of forest-trees, trained high up, forming a canopy above by the joining of the branches at the top, and leaving a clear view beneath. Thus located, the effect of this architecture would be very much admired.

First Floor.—A, vestibule, 6 by 6 feet; B, parlor, 14 by 21 feet; C, sitting-room, 14 by 14 feet; D, dining-room, 14 by 14 feet; E, kitchen, 15 feet 6 inches by 17 feet 6 inches; F, china-closet; G, porch floor; H, back porch.

Second Floor.—J, bath-room, 6 by 10 feet; K, dressing-room, 6 by 6 feet; L, L, L, L, chambers: 14 by 21 feet; 14 by 18 feet 6 inches; 14 by 14 feet; 11 feet 6 inches by 15 feet 6 inches.

DESIGN XLVII.

Model Residence.

FIRST FLOOR.

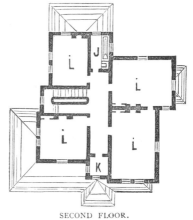

SECOND FLOOR.

DESIGN XLVIII.

A MODEL RESIDENCE.

THIS is a design for a cheap building: almost square, yet broken in such a manner as will add to its apparent size, with trifling expense over a square house. The exterior has but little ornament, yet it is made pretty by the use of proper proportion of its straight lines, showing that beauty is not entirely dependent on ornament, but on the relation of sizes one to the other. The plan contains four fine rooms on each floor, and without the loss of space in forming irregular shapes, as all of the rooms are square, and provided with the same requirements for comfort as larger and more expensive houses. The rooms are all well lighted by large French sash, and they can be thoroughly heated and ventilated. The porch across the front, and bay at the side, are indispensable for comfort and convenience. It can be built for between $3000 and $4000.

First Floor.—A, front porch; B, hall, 6 feet; C, parlor, 12 by 16 feet 7 inches; D, sitting-room, 12 by 12 feet; E, dining-room, 12 by 13 feet; F, kitchen, 12 by 12 feet.

Second Floor.—H, chamber, 12 by 11 feet 6 inches; I, chamber, 12 by 11 feet 6 inches; K, chamber, 12 by 11 feet 6 inches; L, chamber, 13 by 12 feet 9 inches; N, hall, 6 feet; O, roof.

DESIGN XLVIII.

A Model Residence.

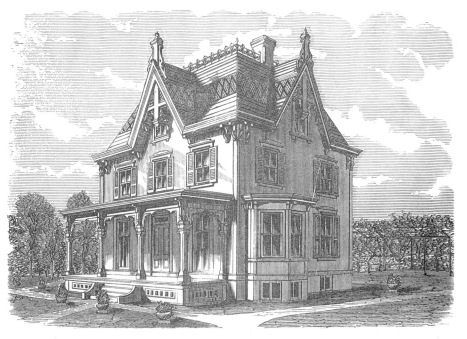

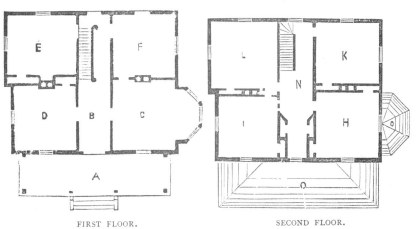

FIRST FLOOR.　　　　SECOND FLOOR.

DESIGN XLIX.

AN ELIZABETHAN VILLA.

THIS design is suitable for a suburban residence. Built of bricks, and pointed, or of rubble stone, it would present a grand effect. The cost would be about $27,000. Good proportion is absolutely required for this style of building. It must be self-evident to most persons that to attempt to build a house of the pretensions of this design without the aid of a competent architect would be a madness, as it would evidently result in disappointment and materially detract from its beauty.

First Floor.—A, front porch; B, vestibule; C, hall, 12 feet wide; D, parlor, 18 by 38 feet; E, library, 19 by 19 feet; F, dining-room, 16 by 31 feet; G, conservatory; H, kitchen, 16 by 18 feet; I, scullery, 10 by 16 feet; J, back stairway; K, pantry; L, china-closet; M, porch.

Second Floor.—P, bath-room; Q, dressing-room; R, chambers.

DESIGN XLIX.

An Elizabethan Villa.

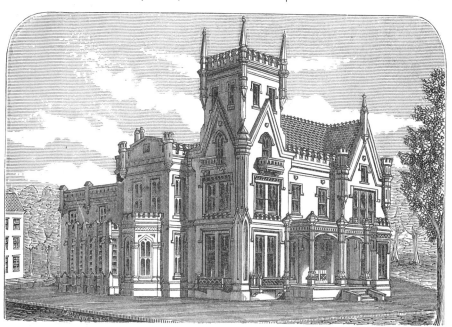

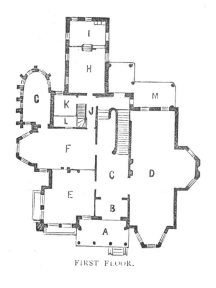

FIRST FLOOR.

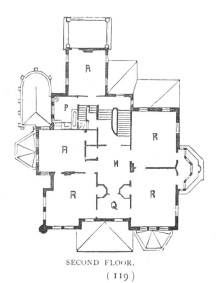

SECOND FLOOR.

DESIGN L.

THIS design is intended to meet the wants of many who are anxious to build a square, compact house. It can be built of either wood, brick, or stone. The kitchen wing is intended to be only two stories high, with a flat roof.

The entrance doors are on each side, by a hall running across the whole, which leaves the parlor and sitting-room occupy the whole. The entrances are by the side porches. The plan works admirably well, and the whole is quite a success. It was built in the vicinity of Pittsburg.

It contains: B, a parlor, 15 by 25 feet; C, a library, 15 by 18 feet; D, sitting-room, 15 by 25 feet; E, dining-room, 15 by 23 feet; kitchen, 12 by 18 feet; with large pantry, and back stairway. The chambers in second story correspond in size to the rooms below. The building will cost for its erection from $7000 to $10,000, according to the style of finish and expensive character of materials.

DESIGN L.

Suburban Residence.

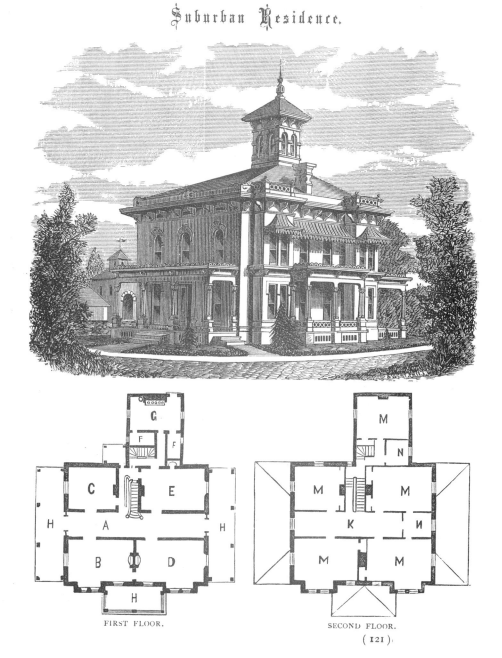

FIRST FLOOR.

SECOND FLOOR.

DESIGN LI.

THIS building is in the Italian style of architecture, and will be found to possess many desirable features. The plan is compact, airy, and easy of access to all its parts. For a physician, lawyer, or gentleman doing business at his residence, it will be found very convenient. If built of pointed stone-work, suitable to its pretensions, it will cost, at Philadelphia, $7500. The porches upon each side, in consequence of the arched heads to openings, look low, and spoil the general effect. By a proper adjustment of them the design will be quite desirable.

First Floor.—A, porch; B, vestibule; C, office; D, stair-hall; E, dining-room; F, parlor; G, kitchen; H, scullery; I, pantry; J, porch.

Second Floor.—N, roofs; L, chambers; M, bath-room; O, stair-landing.

DESIGN LI.

Italian Villa.

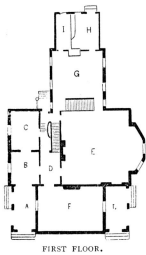

FIRST FLOOR.

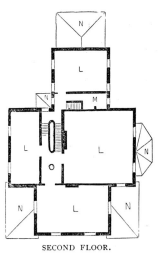

SECOND FLOOR.

DESIGN LII.

SUBURBAN RESIDENCE, GRECIAN STYLE.

THIS design is in the Grecian style of architecture, and will make a very comfortable and pretty residence. The building is drawn for frame, and, in adapting it to stone, it would have to be made larger. It contains on the first floor a suite of three rooms, water-closet, shed, and pantry. The second story contains four bed-rooms. It is of a style of architecture that needs to be carefully proportioned, to obtain much beauty. It has breadth in its proportions, and the form and size of its details will either make it beautiful or hideous. This house will cost $2000, if built of frame; $2500, of bricks.

First Floor.—A, kitchen, 15 by 16 feet; B, living-room, 20 by 16 feet; C, bed-room, 15 by 15 feet; D, wood-shed, 8 by 16 feet; E, water-closet, 4 by 4 feet; F, passage to cellar and wood-shed; H, front porch, 5 by 10 feet.

Second Floor.—K, bed-room, 9 by 14 feet; L, bed-room, 9 by 16 feet; M, bed-room, 8 by 9 feet; N, bed-room, 9 by 11 feet.

DESIGN LII.

Suburban Residence, in the Grecian Style.

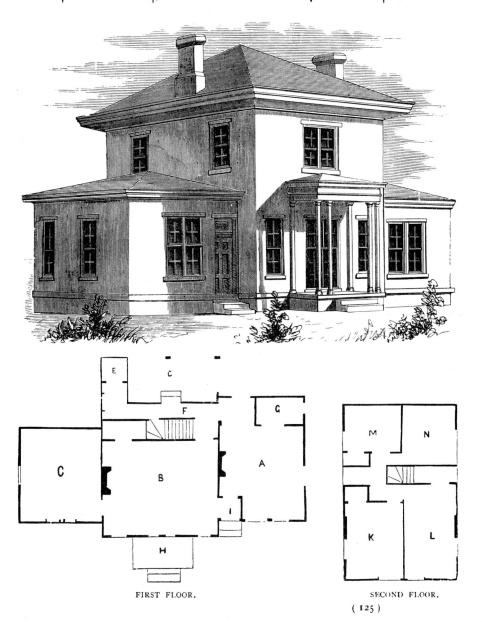

FIRST FLOOR.

SECOND FLOOR.

(125)

DESIGN LIII.

SUBURBAN RESIDENCE.

THIS is a design for a mansion with first-class accommodations. It can be made a grand building, of an imposing character. It was designed to be finished with stucco upon the outside, but this is liable to crack and fall off in a few years; it being impossible to make it stand all the changes of our climate. We would advise bricks, laid with flush joints, rubbed down and painted; or stone, laid in courses, with vertical joints. It will admirably suit a situation where the grounds are low in the rear, as the kitchen, scullery, etc., are in the basement story. Dumbwaiters and free servant-ways must be provided for in such a building. Should we make the detail drawings, it can be built for $10,000, and will have an air of refinement and style. Peculiarly adapted to an old-established family of refinement and ease. High stories, ample doors and windows, but plain, and in true proportion.

The first floor has: A, grand hall, 12 by 36 feet; B, parlor, 15 by 30 feet, with a circular bay, 14 by 8 feet; C, dining-room, 15 by 23 feet; D, sitting-room, 11 by 15 feet; E, reception-room, 8 by 12 feet; F, small office, 8 by 12 feet.

The second floor has seven chambers marked M; bath- and bed-rooms, K; L, stair-landing.

First floor, 15 feet high; second, 14 feet. The roof of boiled iron, patent seams, with cornice of galvanized iron; the top balcony of wood, painted and sanded.

DESIGN LIII.

Suburban Residence.

FIRST FLOOR.

SECOND FLOOR.

DESIGN LIV.

SUBURBAN RESIDENCE.

THIS style of a house contains the spirit of a Philadelphia building. The plans are similar to those put up in solid phalanx, miles of which are built with little deviation. The grounds should be little broken as possible. Level grade, smooth grass, fine, wide, red walks, and all kept cleanly and prim around, it will not be hard to guess the disposition and religious feelings of the owner. It is intended for two houses, —so built that they will form in appearance one large building. They are conveniently arranged, and have a very agreeable appearance. They will cost about $6000 or $8000 each, and are suitable for villages or for suburban residences where width of lot does not exceed fifty feet.

First Floor.—A, parlor, 13 by 26 feet; B, hall, 3 feet 6 inches wide; C, dining-room, 12 by 20 feet; D, kitchen, 12 by 14 feet.

There are four comfortable chambers on second story, with closets, etc.

DESIGN LIV.

Suburban Residence.

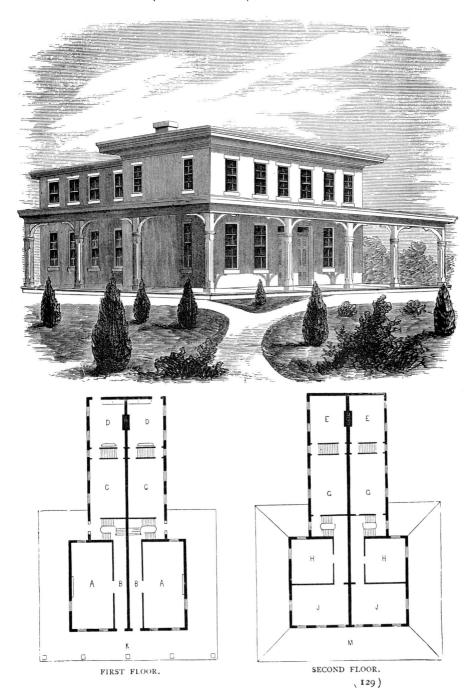

FIRST FLOOR.

SECOND FLOOR.

DESIGN LV.

AN AMERICAN COTTAGE.

THIS design is intended to be built of stone. The peculiar shape of the plan renders it extremely fine for a summer seat, as the wings catch the winds, and render it very airy and comfortable. The proportions of the rooms are large, making a very beautiful and comfortable summer residence. The roof is of shingles or slate, and the superstructure rubble masonry, pointed. It can be built for $7000, frame; $8000, brick; $9000, stone. It ranks high for the style of its architecture and proportion. It would require a large lot if used as a suburban design. One hundred feet would not be crowded, but if less than that, other evolutions will be advisable. The accommodations are quite large; much less will be found advisable, unless the families are proportional.

A, parlor, 16 by 30 feet; B, porch; C, main hall; 16 by 16 feet; D, sitting-room, 16 by 16 feet; E, dining-room, 13 by 16 feet; F, kitchen, 16 by 18 feet.

The second floor contains four fine chambers; the third floor, two attic rooms.

DESIGN LV.

An American Cottage.

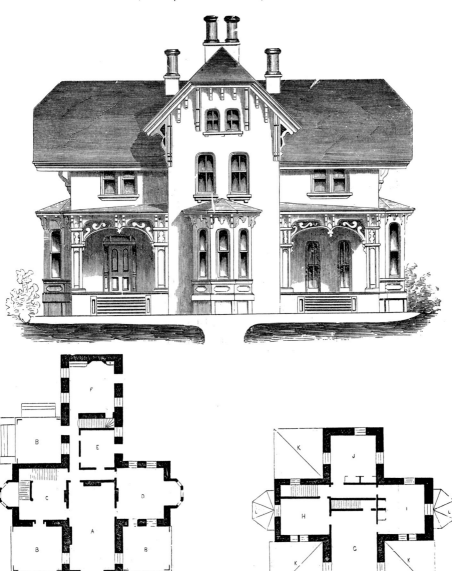

FIRST FLOOR.

SECOND FLOOR.

(131)

DESIGN LVI.

SUBURBAN RESIDENCE.

THIS house was designed for the authoress, Mrs. Randolph, with careful attention to detail and finish. We have no hesitation in saying that it is a most desirable residence. A noticeable feature in the design is the carriage-porch, which is obviously of importance, as it affords shelter, while, by the addition of a railing, the roof is converted into a neat veranda, and communicates with the front chambers of the second story.

Entering the first floor through the carriage-porch, one passes through the tower hall into the main hall, which gives access to the parlor, dining-room, and main staircase. The library communicates with the conservatory; the breakfast- and dining-rooms, as also kitchen, pantry, and wash-house, being likewise upon this floor.

This house is intended to be erected of brick, with stone window-dressings; the roofs of slate or tin. It could be built for $18,000.

First Floor.—P, parlor; B, library; F, tower hall; H, main hall; C, conservatory; I, breakfast-room; D, dining-room; G, porch; V, veranda; K, kitchen; E, pantry; W, wash-room; A, carriage-porch.

Second Floor.—V, veranda; U, principal chamber and bath-room; X, chamber; S, closet; O, main hall; Y, boudoir; H, veranda; A, roof of porch; Z, chamber; N, back chamber; M, F, J, bed-rooms.

DESIGN LVI.

Suburban Residence.

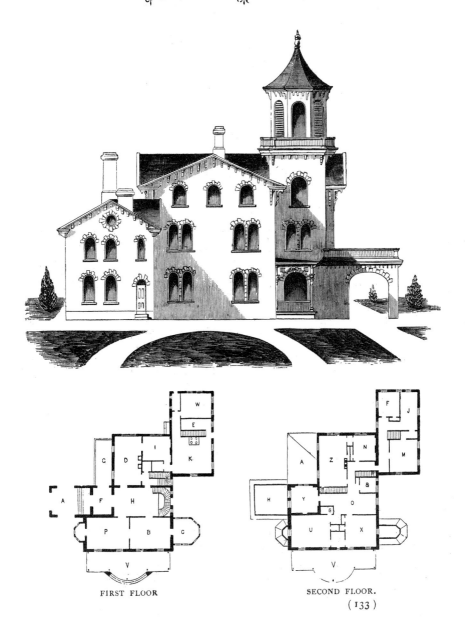

FIRST FLOOR

SECOND FLOOR.

(133)

DESIGN LVII.

ITALIAN VILLA.

THIS villa is designed for a large family, and will be found to contain ample and superior accommodations. It was constructed of stone; the cornices, brackets, porches, and all external wood-work painted and sanded in color, harmonious with that of the building. The porch roofs are to be covered with tin. The main hall, which is of fine proportions, gives access to the parlor, reception-room, dining-room, and stair-hall; in the parlor is a piano recess. The breakfast-room opens by means of doors into both dining-room and kitchen: access being also had to it from the stair-hall. Two water-closets adjoin the kitchen.

Upon the second floor the main hall gives access to the four principal chambers and stair-hall. The sitting-room communicates with the bath-room and water-closets. Cost, $10,000. To parties desiring to build a design similar to this, we will state that we can make such changes in it that will much improve the whole effect. The brackets are bad and clumsy; the circular-headed windows spoil their proportion. Aside from this, the design is acceptable and the plans are good. For those who desire the kitchen so placed, a back stair can be introduced by adding three feet greater depth.

First Floor.—P, parlor, 30 by 15 feet; H, main hall, 10 feet; R, reception-room, 15 by 15 feet; D, dining-room, 15 by 15 feet; B, breakfast-room, 12 by 14 feet; K, kitchen, 12 by 14 feet; S, stair-hall, 10 by 12 feet; C, piano recess, 10 by 12 feet; F, porch, 10 feet; A, back porch, 10 feet; W C, water-closet.

Second Floor.—C, four principal chambers, 15 by 15 feet; H, main hall, 10 feet; G, stair-hall, 10 by 12 feet; M, roof of porch, 11 feet; N, roof of porch, back, 11 feet; B, sitting-room, 10 by 13 feet; T, bath-room, 7 by 7 feet 6 inches.

DESIGN LVII.

Italian Villa.

FIRST FLOOR.

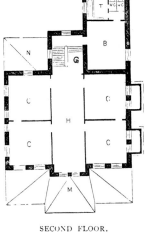

SECOND FLOOR.

DESIGN LVIII.

ITALIAN VILLA.

ITALIAN mansion, two stories, and an attic story for servants. The building is intended to be built of bricks, painted. It has a conservatory, a bay in library, fine porches, first-class accommodations throughout. It can be built for about $8oco. Tin roofs; well finished interiorly.

First Floor.—A, porch, 8 feet wide: B, main hall, 9 feet; C, parlor, 14 feet 6 inches by 21 feet; D, library, 14 feet 6 inches by 13 feet 6 inches; E, conservatory; F, back porch, 6 feet; G, kitchen, 13 feet 6 inches by 18 feet; H, dining-room, 25 by 14 feet 6 inches; I, sitting-room, 15 by 17 feet 6 inches; K, side porch.

Second Floor.—L, chamber, 14 feet 6 inches by 17 feet 6 inches; M, dressing-room, 9 by S feet 6 inches; N, chamber, 14 feet 6 inches by 15 feet 6 inches; O, chamber, 17 feet 6 inches by 14 feet 6 inches; P, hall, 9 feet; R, chamber, 20 feet 6 inches by 14 feet 6 inches; S, bath-room; T, bed-room, 13 feet 6 inches by 10 feet; U, veranda; V, veranda.

DESIGN LVIII.

Italian Villa.

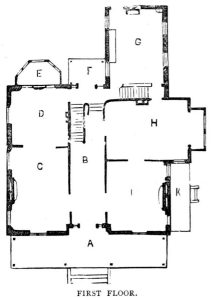

FIRST FLOOR.

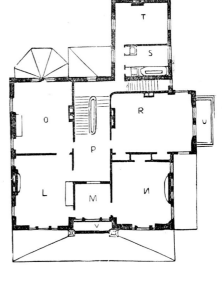

SECOND FLOOR.

DESIGN LIX.

SUBURBAN RESIDENCE, ITALIAN STYLE.

THIS house was built for Dr. J. K. Lee, Chestnut Street, West Philadelphia, and is very generally admired. The house is built of brown stone, with roof of tin, and is not less attractive than comfortable.

The accommodations provided for, by the plan of the principal floor, consist of a fine projecting veranda porch, which gives access to the hall, office, drawing-room, dining-room, and stair-hall. The dining-room and parlor have each a bay-window, decorated with stained glass. The accommodations for the culinary department are ample, there being both a kitchen and an out-kitchen. There is also a spacious pantry upon this floor.

This house was built in 1866, and cost, when completed, between $6000 and $8000.

First Floor—1, reception-hall, 8 by 10 feet; 2, office, 10 by 12 feet; 3, stair-hall, 7 feet; 4, parlor, 16 by 22 feet; 5, dining-room, 15 by 20 feet 6 inches; 6, kitchen, 16 by 16 feet 6 inches; 7, pantry, 7 feet 6 inches by 4 feet 6 inches; 8, out-kitchen, 9 feet 6 inches by 7 feet 6 inches; 9, 10, porch.

Second Floor.—11, dressing-room, 10 by 9 feet 6 inches; 12, bath-room, 10 by 11 feet; 13, entry; 14, closet; 16, chamber, 16 by 22 feet; 17, chamber, 10 by 13 feet; 18, hall; 19, chamber, 10 by 14 feet; 20, closet; 21, nursery, 16 feet 6 inches by 16 feet; 22, 23, veranda.

DESIGN LIX.

Suburban Residence, in the Italian Style.

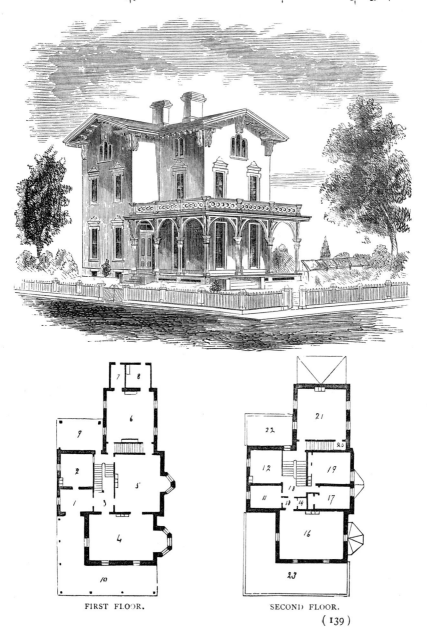

FIRST FLOOR.

SECOND FLOOR.

DESIGN LX.

SUBURBAN VILLA.

This design is in the Italian style, Americanized. That it cannot be otherwise will appear from the following reasons: it is not Roman, as most of its details are Greek; neither is it Athenian, for some of its windows have arched heads. It is covered with a Tuscan roof, which is Roman. An Italian composition adapts it to the climate, wants, and customs of the United States, to which all the internal arrangements can be made to suit.

The building is of a character that demands an elevated situation, as it will appear to better advantage, and harmonize well with cultivated lawns and moderately varied grounds. A wide terrace will be necessary for a base, as shown in the perspective. The accommodations are extensive; the chambers are sufficiently numerous, spacious, airy, and conveniently arranged. The verandas make abundant provision for shade. It will cost $12,000, if well built, at present range of prices. The stairway must be lighted from above.

First Floor.—A, portico, 10 feet; B, lobby, 12 by 15 feet; C, library, 12 by 21 feet; D, kitchen, 15 by 18 feet; E, drawing-room, 16 by 25 feet; F, back parlor, 16 by 26 feet; G, hall, 15 feet; H, dining-room, 16 by 27 feet; I, billiard-room, 15 by 22 feet; K, porch, 8 feet.

Second Floor.—L, veranda; M, dressing-room, 15 by 22 feet; N, hall, 15 feet; O, chamber, 16 by 25 feet; P, chamber, 12 by 21 feet; R, chamber, 16 by 27 feet; S, chamber, 16 by 26 feet; T, chamber, 15 by 22 feet; U, veranda.

DESIGN LX.

𝕾𝖚𝖇𝖚𝖗𝖇𝖆𝖓 𝖁𝖎𝖑𝖑𝖆.

FIRST FLOOR.

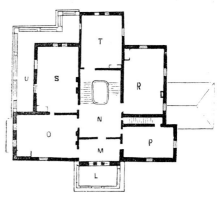

SECOND FLOOR.

DESIGN LXI.

VILLAGE OR SUBURBAN RESIDENCE.

THIS design can be built of either stone or frame, and covered with slate or shingles. It contains three floors, and has four rooms on each floor. It is capable of making a very beautiful building if carried out according to the particular feeling and proportion embodied therein. There is a front and a rear porch, and two side porches, whose roofs are to be covered with tin. The chimneys are to be finished with terra-cotta tops, and ample provision is made for ventilation. Upon the first floor the front porch gives access to the vestibule and hall; the hall communicates with the parlor and library; the dining-room and kitchen are conveniently arranged with reference to access from the one to the other; the side porches extend the whole depth of the house. Upon the second and third floors are four chambers to the floor,—spacious and well ventilated. The cost of the building is $6000.

First Floor.—1, front porch; 2, vestibule; 3, hall; 4, library; 5, dining-room; 6, parlor; 7, kitchen; 8, rear porch; 9, side porch.

Second Floor.—10, veranda; 11, 11, closets; 12, boudoir; 13, 14, 15, 16, chambers.

DESIGN LXI.

Village or Suburban Residence.

FIRST FLOOR.

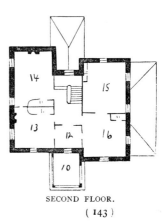

SECOND FLOOR.

(143)

DESIGN LXII.

RESIDENCE IN THE ITALIAN STYLE.

THIS design has a commodious and well-arranged interior. The roofs are intended for tin, and the superstructure of stone. It has a fine porch, projecting and bay-windows, with a look-out or cupola. These designs can be modified by the architect, to suit the means of persons wishing to build. Porches are the most expensive kind of ornament, but even they must be very expensive to materially alter the cost of a good building. Porches cost at this time about $10 for each running foot, measured along the frieze. Bay-windows cost about the same over the plain wall and its windows. It is the internal accommodation that produces this; plumbing is a very heavy item, if fully performed up to the fashion and improvements of the day; heating also is a matter of considerable expense, together with marble, stucco work, and stairways. It will cost $20,000.

First Floor.—1, parlor, 18 by 36 feet; 2, porch; 3, vestibule, 12 by 12 feet; 4, conservatory, 12 by 12 feet; 5, library, 12 by 16 feet; 6, hall, 12 feet; 7, dining-room, 16 by 27 feet; 8, breakfast-room, 15 by 15 feet; 9, kitchen, 18 by 12 feet; 10, scullery, 18 by 12 feet; 11, porch.

Second Floor.—12, principal chamber, 18 by 36 feet; 13, hall; 14, chamber, 16 by 16 feet; 15, dressing-room, 8 by 12 feet; 16, chamber, 16 by 16 feet; 17, chamber, 15 by 15 feet; 18, 19, bed-rooms, 10 by 18 feet; 20, bath room, 9 by 14 feet; 21, linen-closet, 8 by 8 feet; 22, veranda.

DESIGN LXII.

Residence in the Italian Style.

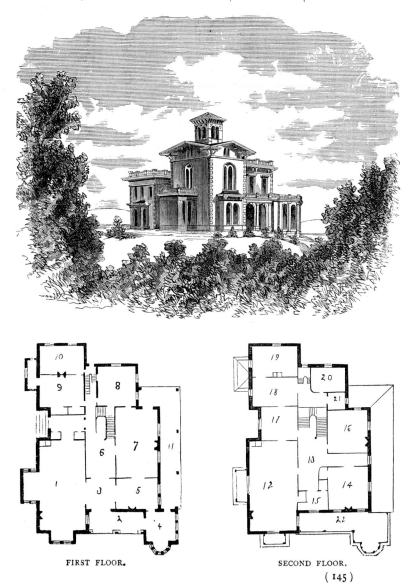

FIRST FLOOR.

SECOND FLOOR.

(145)

DESIGN LXIII.

SUBURBAN RESIDENCE.

THIS design is quite perfect in its plan, and contains all the requirements for internal comforts, as well as considerable exterior attraction. It is of a style which is much used, and its beauty will depend upon the proportion of its parts, and the correctness of its details. Cost, with all improvements, $8000.

Many mechanics throughout the country imagine that they can adopt what appears to them as beautiful in one house, and by transferring (or rather *apparently* transferring) it to their own, produce the same effect. Persons are continually sacrificing style, finish, and proportion in their buildings, in order to save architects' fees. We have buildings adjacent to Philadelphia that will sell for three times their cost; and there are many which have been built without the aid of an architect that will not realize their cost.

First Floor.—A, parlor, 13 by 30 feet 3 inches; B, hall, 13 by 13 feet; C, sitting-room, 13 by 16 feet 9 inches; D, dining-room, 12 by 24 feet 6 inches; E, kitchen, 11 feet 6 inches by 16 feet; F, scullery, 8 feet 9 inches by 14 feet; G, H, porches.

Second Floor.—I, chamber, 15 feet 10 inches by 11 feet 8 inches; J, chamber, 16 feet 10 inches by 13 feet; K, chamber, 13 feet 8 inches by 13 feet; L, chamber, 12 by 20 feet; M, chamber, 11 feet 3 inches by 16 feet 8 inches.

DESIGN LXIII.

Suburban Residence.

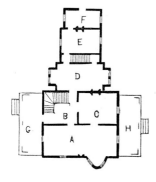

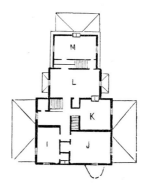

FIRST FLOOR.

SECOND FLOOR.

(147)

DESIGN LXIV.

ITALIAN VILLA.

THIS design, which is in the Italian style, is both commodious and well-arranged internally. The roofs are of tin, with a superstructure of stone. The building will cost, at the present price of materials and labor, from $20,000 to $25,000.

The first floor contains a large vestibule, hall, spacious drawing-room, dining-room, sitting-room, library, and music-room. The kitchen departments are placed below.

The second floor contains four commodious chambers, a boudoir, bath-room, and dressing-room.

The height of the floors is 14 feet and 12 feet.

First Floor.—1, front porch; 2, vestibule, 12 by 12 feet; 3, hall; 4, drawing-room, 23 feet 3 inches by 29 feet; 5, library, 15 by 15 feet; 6, dining-room, 26 feet 6 inches by 16 feet; 7, sitting-room, 15 feet 9 inches by 22 feet; 8, rear porch; 9, music-room, 18 feet 9 inches by 12 feet; 10, area.

Second Floor.—11, veranda; 12, boudoir, 15 by 15 feet; 13, chamber, 23 feet 3 inches by 24 feet; 14, dressing-room, 12 by 12 feet; 15, hall; 16, chamber, 26 feet 6 inches by 16 feet; 17, chamber, 15 feet 9 inches by 17 feet; 18, chamber, 18 feet 9 inches by 17 feet; 19, bath-room, 7 by 7 feet.

DESIGN LXIV.

Italian Villa.

FIRST FLOOR

SECOND FLOOR.

DESIGN LXV.

ITALIAN VILLA.

THIS design is one of those imposing buildings which are fully up to the advanced tastes of the age. It would suit well upon a headland, looking out upon a bay, with gentle sloping surroundings. Much money is wasted yearly in ineffective ornament and badly-proportioned buildings, ill adapted to the situation and surrounding scenery. Buildings should always be proportioned according to the open or close character of the view, as well as the distance to be seen from. In designing a building two things must be borne in mind : one, that it is to be looked at; the other, that it is to be looked from. The side exposed to the principal approach should have the greatest attention. Many parts of buildings it would be utter ignorance to ornament highly, as it draws attention to them more particularly. Too much poverty in such places calls the attention, and makes them prominent. The only correct mode is to treat them subjectly. Designing a building is like a battle upon canvas of color, each part striving for supremacy. This is truthful in material nature, as it is in man and animals—all a strife for life.

The architect, like all others, should make an honest distribution of his forces, or he starves one part and overloads with fatness the others. Give each its just due, and they will all be quiet; no wrangling; but one beautiful, peaceful, harmonious assemblage, all coming forward with their little gifts, giving them quietly and freely. Such is harmony.

First Floor.—A, conservatory, 16 feet 6 inches by 21 feet; B, parlor, 16 by 31 feet 6 inches; C, vestibule, 12 by 12 feet; D, hall, 12 feet wide; E, sitting-room, 25 feet 6 inches by 16 feet 3 inches; F, library, 11 by 6 feet; G, dining-room, 14 feet 9 inches by 28 feet; H, store-room, 10 by 10 feet; I, kitchen, 18 by 18 feet; J, scullery, 11 by 18 feet; K, L, porches; M, N, side porches.

DESIGN LXV.

Italian Villa.

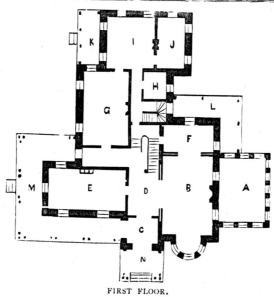

FIRST FLOOR.

DESIGN LXVI.

SUBURBAN RESIDENCE.

THIS design was drawn for the Hon. Andrew G. Curtin, at Bellefonte, Pa. It is of mountain freestone, laid in rubble-work, pointed with white mortar, with a neat black line; the wood-work outside painted and sanded the color of the stone; the interior arranged with regard to comfort as well as elegance. The plumbing is very complete, and mirror-back washstands and other improvements are placed in the house. Heating is accomplished by means of an improved heater, low-down grates, etc. Preferring inside finish of best quality and workmanship to outside show, the building is but two stories high, in order to obtain this result without exceeding the desired amount. This house cost $27,000.

First Floor.—1, front porch; 2, vestibule, 6 feet 8 inches by 9 feet; 3, parlor, 26 feet 2 inches by 22 feet 10 inches; 4, hall; 5, reception-room, 15 feet 7 inches by 15 feet 10 inches; 6, dining-room, 18 feet 4 inches by 23 feet 6 inches; 7, library, 16 by 26 feet; 8, china-closet, 4 feet 3 inches by 4 feet 5 inches; 9, pantry, 4 feet 3 inches by 8 feet 4 inches; 10, store-room, 3 feet 9 inches by 5 feet; 11, kitchen, 16 by 17 feet; 12, scullery; 13, porch.

Second Floor.—14, balcony; 15, boudoir, 9 feet 6 inches by 11 feet 6 inches; 16, chamber, 15 feet 8 inches by 15 feet 11 inches; 17, chamber, 21 by 23 feet; 18, dressing-room, 5 feet 5 inches by 9 feet; 19, chamber, 26 feet 4 inches by 16 feet; 20, chamber, 18 feet 6 inches by 24 feet; 21, bath-room, 5 feet 6 inches by 12 feet; 22, chamber, 12 feet 10 inches by 16 feet 4 inches; 23, nursery, 19 feet 6 inches by 15 feet 10 inches.

DESIGN LXVI.

Suburban Residence.

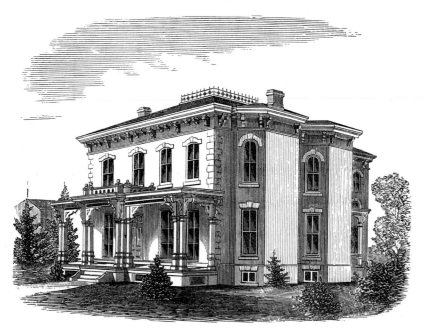

FIRST FLOOR.

SECOND FLOOR.

(153)

DESIGN LXVII.

SUBURBAN RESIDENCE.

THIS design was intended for a gentleman in Alleghany City, and possesses a grandeur rarely obtained. It is intended to be of brick, painted; and its particular feature is the glass-domed hall, with a double elliptical stairway, lighted by stained glass. The library is, according to desire, one of the best rooms in the house, delightfully situated, and, when furnished with book-cases, statuary, and other appropriate ornaments, it will have great attractions. The ground upon which the house is to stand was such that it is very desirable in this instance to place the scullery, wash-rooms, etc., in the basement story. The house is heated by means of large heater, low-down grates, etc.

First Floor.—A, main hall, 12 feet wide; B, parlor, 16 by 26 feet; C, dining-room, 16 by 26 feet 3 inches; D, music-room, 12 feet 10 inches by 11 feet 3 inches; E, office, 12 feet 3 inches by 11 feet 10 inches; F, library, 20 feet 3 inches by 21 feet 3 inches; G, kitchen, 17 feet 10 inches by 18 feet 9 inches; H, servants' hall; I, pantry; J, closet; K, stair hall.

Second Floor.—L, chamber, 16 feet 3 inches by 18 feet 10 inches; M, chamber, 15 feet 6 inches by 19 feet 5 inches; N, chamber, 17 feet 6 inches by 19 feet 5 inches; O, bath-room, 6 feet 9 inches by 9 feet 10 inches; P, chamber, 14 feet 2 inches by 16 feet 3 inches: Q, chamber, 16 feet 3 inches by 20 feet 6 inches; R, chamber, 13 feet 3 inches by 19 feet 10 inches; S, stair-hall.

DESIGN LXVII.

Suburban Residence.

FIRST FLOOR.

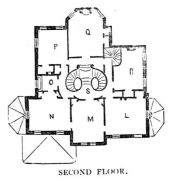

SECOND FLOOR.

DESIGN LXVIII.

SUBURBAN RESIDENCE.

THIS house possesses a noble appearance, without having an excess of ornament. It could be built for $8000, plainly finished in the interior. It is drawn from a point eighty feet distant. Being in a diagonal course from the house, it would place the house about sixty feet from the front of the lot. The lot should be about seventy-five feet front. Placed in such a position, on raised ground, about six feet above the road, it would have the appearance as shown here.

First Floor.—1, vestibule, 9 by 9 feet; 2, hall, 12 by 8 feet; 3, parlor, 16 by 22 feet, 4-foot bay-window; 4, library, 15 by 15 feet; 5, dining-room, 16 by 22 feet; 6, sitting-room, 12 by 16 feet; 7, kitchen, 15 by 15 feet; 8, out-kitchen, 10 by 15 feet; 9, front porch, 10 feet; 10, side porch, 10 feet.

Second Floor.—11, boudoir, 9 by 9 feet; 12, chamber, 16 by 22 feet; 13, chamber, 15 by 15 feet; 14, chamber, 16 by 22 feet; 15, chamber, 12 by 16 feet; 16, hall, 8 and 12 feet; 17, bath-room, 8 by 12 feet; 18, bed-room, 15 by 16 feet 6 inches.

DESIGN LXVIII.

Suburban Residence.

FIRST FLOOR.

SECOND FLOOR.

(157)

DESIGN LXIX.

SUBURBAN RESIDENCE.

THIS design was made for a gentleman in Belle-fonte, a thriving town in Centre Co., Pa., where we have a number of first-class residences, costing from $5000 to $30,000 each; and we refer to all of them as being beautiful, whilst differing in their proportions and styles. This house will cost between $20,000 and $30,000.

First Floor.—A, vestibule; B, hall, 12 feet 3 inches; C, parlor, 27 feet 3 inches by 38 feet 9 inches; D, library, 17 feet 9 inches by 19 feet 7 inches; E, dining-room, 31 feet 6 inches by 16 feet; H, butler's pantry, 9 feet 4 inches by 5 feet 7 inches; I, china-closet, 9 feet 3 inches by 6 feet 4 inches; J, front porch; K, porch; kitchen, 16 by 18 feet; scullery, 16 by 12 feet.

Second Floor.—L, chamber, 19 feet 7 inches by 17 feet 9 inches; M, chamber, 18 feet 6 inches by 19 feet; M, balcony; N, chamber, 18 feet 6 inches by 19 feet; O, chamber, 20 feet 6 inches by 16 feet; P, chamber, 16 feet 6 inches by 16 feet; Q, bath-room, 9 feet 9 inches by 6 feet; S, observatory; other bath-room, 9 feet 9 inches by 4 feet 9 inches.

DESIGN LXIX.

Suburban Residence.

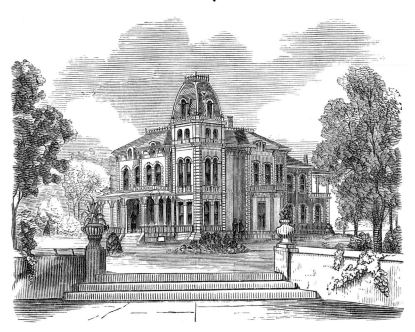

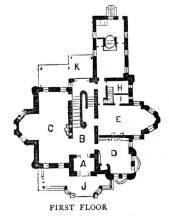

FIRST FLOOR

SECOND FLOOR.

(159

DESIGN LXX.

MANSION IN THE ELIZABETHAN STYLE.

THIS design is drawn in the Elizabethan style of architecture, Italianized. It is presented with a view to show what amount of beauty should be visible in the piling up of a quantity of material and labor. It can be executed in fine style for $150,000, and might vie with many of the castles in Europe that cost as many pounds. Here we have a blending of a number of fine architectural effects, obtaining largeness and importance of appearance, without the almshouse architecture that we see displayed in many of equal size and cost all over the country. The design, with modifications, would make a very fine ladies' seminary.

Dimensions.—A, principal hall, 15 feet 6 inches; A, stair-hall, 17 feet wide; B, parlor, 19 feet 6 inches by 35 feet; C, drawing-room, 43 by 26 feet; D, dining-room, 37 by 40 feet; E, sitting-room, 19 feet 6 inches by 35 feet; L, library, 25 by 26 feet; G, ladies' room, 25 by 13 feet; H, hothouse, 12 by 24 feet; I, billiard-room, 15 by 32 feet; J, rotunda, 24 by 24 feet; K, smoking-room, 17 by 22 feet; L, servants' room, 16 by 22 feet; M, breakfast-room, 16 by 29 feet 6 inches; N, kitchen, 25 feet by 29 feet 6 inches; O, wash-house and scullery, 18 by 34 feet; P, tower, 11 by 11 feet; Q, porches, 17 and 11 feet; R, tower; S, pavilion; T, arcade; U, hall passages.

DESIGN LXX.

Mansion in the Elizabethan Style.

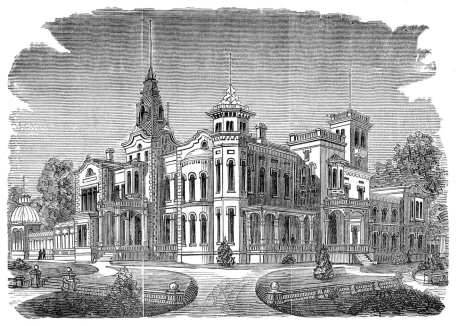

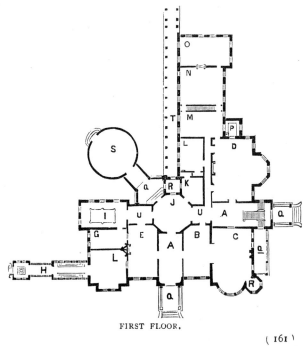

FIRST FLOOR.

DESIGN LXXI.

ITALIAN VILLA.

THIS design is in the Italian style, and its situation is ninety feet back, and viewed from a point six feet above the ground and one hundred and five feet from its nearest part.

It contains beautiful and ample apartments, and possesses externally a noble appearance. There is an abundance of veranda accommodation, which renders it a very desirable residence for the summer season.

It should have a broad, unbroken lawn in front, and in the rear some stately trees should be found, forming a grove, and making a background suitable for the character of the villa. It can be built of earthen bricks, or of stone, laid broken range and pointed; in which case it will look more noble than if of bricks painted. The building can be completely finished with bath, heaters, marble mantels, and fine stucco centre-pieces and cornices, for $12,000, around Philadelphia. The roof is intended to be covered with slates.

First Floor.—A, vestibule, 11 by 11 feet; B, parlor, 15 by 21 feet; C, library, 15 by 11 feet; D, dining-room, 17 by 26 feet; E, kitchen, 15 by 22 feet; F, pantry; G, scullery, 15 by 15 feet; H, china-closet; I, front porch; J, side porch; K, back shed; hall, 11 feet wide.

DESIGN LXXI.

Italian Villa.

FIRST FLOOR.

DESIGN LXXII.

AMERICAN BRACKETED VILLA.

THIS building is of so beautiful and attractive a kind as to require no further embellishments. The arrangement of the front porch, and the perfect proportion of the various parts, afford as grand an outline as could be obtained by the more costly style of projecting wings. The plan contains all the requirements of the times, and is capable of being added to, or reduced, without materially altering the appearance of the whole. The back stairway and conservatory might, for instance, be dispensed with; or a kitchen might be added in the rear of back stairs, and the space now marked kitchen taken for a bed-room. The building would look well of either wood or brick; if of the latter, it should be rubbed down and painted. It would cost about $8000.

First Floor.—A, entrance-porch; B, hall, 8 feet wide; C, parlor, 14 feet 3 inches by 20 feet; D, sitting-room, 14 by 14 feet; E, dining-room, 16 by 24 feet; F, kitchen, 16 by 16 feet; H, porches; J, conservatory.

Second Floor.—K, chamber, 14 by 20 feet; L, chamber, 14 by 14 feet; M, chamber, 16 by 24 feet; N, chamber, 9 by 14 feet; O, hall, 8 feet wide; P, sewing-room, 8 by 8 feet; R, bath-room, 5 feet 2 inches by 10 feet.

DESIGN LXXII.

American Bracketed Villa.

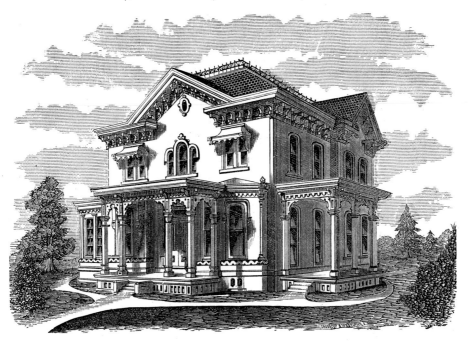

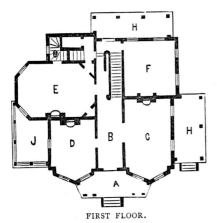

FIRST FLOOR.

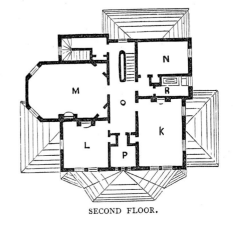

SECOND FLOOR.

DESIGN LXXIII.

ITALIAN VILLA.

This design, which is in the Italian style, is intended for, and admirably adapted to, the wants of a gentleman of a large family. The accommodations are ample, and the interior arrangements exceedingly simple, as will readily be seen by reference to the plans of first and second stories. The exterior, which is intended to be executed in stone, presents a beautiful and chaste appearance, and is capable of a high tone of architectural beauty.

The carriage-porch gives access to the vestibule, which communicates with the parlors and stair-hall. The piano-room and conservatory adjoin the parlors.

The general entrance gives access to the parlor and stair-hall. The rear entrance gives access to the dining-room, breakfast-room, servants' room, and stair-hall. The domestic offices are placed below.

Upon the second floor are four spacious chambers, a dressing-room, and nursery. All the apartments throughout the house are arranged with reference to convenience of access. Cost, $30,000.

First Floor.—A, music-room ; B, parlor ; C, vestibule ; D, parlor ; E, conservatory (it will be observed that these rooms are all separated by drapery, which being withdrawn, one magnificent parlor is formed) ; F, sitting-room ; G, dining-room ; H, stair-hall ; I, breakfast-room ; J, dumb-waiter ; K, china-closet ; L, servants' room ; M, carriage-porch ; N, general entrance ; O, rear entrance ; P, porticos.

Second Floor.—A, roof ; B, nursery ; C, chambers ; D, dressing-room.

DESIGN LXXIII.

Italian Villa.

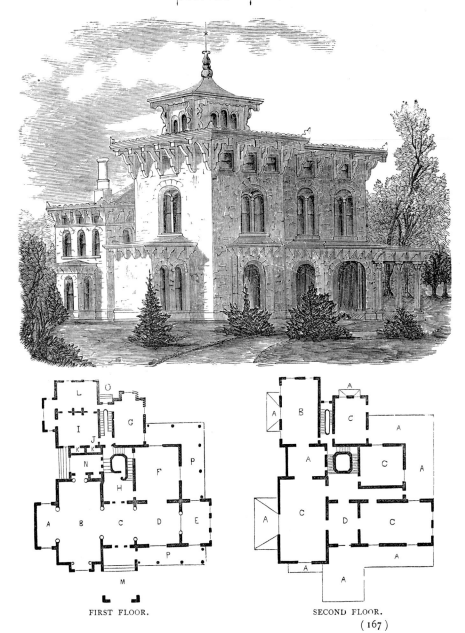

FIRST FLOOR.

SECOND FLOOR.

DESIGN LXXIV.

SCHOOL-HOUSE.

THIS design represents a school-house adapted to a situation in the suburbs of Philadelphia. It is intended to be built of stone, and will furnish ample accommodation for a large number of pupils.

The five rooms marked C on the plan are class-rooms,—23 feet 4 inches by 35 feet in the clear. The remaining space of the two wings is devoted to book-closets and stairways.

DESIGN LXXIV.

School-House.

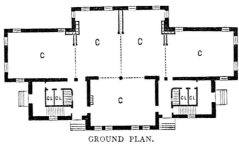

GROUND PLAN.

DESIGN LXXV.

GOTHIC CHURCH.

THIS church is situated upon the East Liberty road, and is about three miles from Pittsburg. It is built of frame, boarded vertically, and battened. The inside is finished with ornamented principal rafters, wrought to a beautiful design, the spaces between them being plastered, and colored azure-blue.

The building contains in its rear wing a lecture-room and school-room, with the walls laid off, and colored in imitation of stone. They have fine high ceilings, and a beautiful bay runs out to the rear, producing an effect which is seldom obtained,—and never in basements. The outside is in full Gothic, the ornaments carved in wood. It is covered with the best quality of slate, and is painted and sanded thoroughly. The whole cost is a little over $15,000. The pews and pulpit are black walnut. This church may be considered a successful attempt at wooden Gothic architecture. It was burned down, but rebuilt as before.

Dimensions.—Church, 52 feet by 37 feet 9 inches; 1, vestibule, 13 feet 3 inches by 12 feet 6 inches ; 2, aisles, 4 feet wide; 3, pulpit; 4, lecture-room, 38 feet 6 inches by 36 feet; 5, infants' school-room, 14 feet 8 inches by 10 feet 6 inches; 6, centre pews, 16 feet long,—accommodating nine persons each; side pews will accommodate four each.

DESIGN LXXV.

Gothic Church.

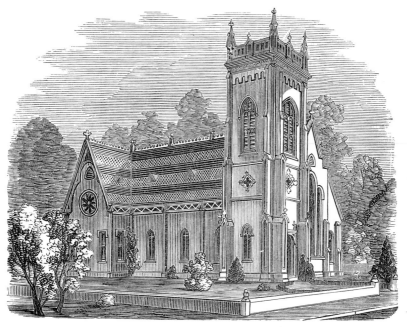

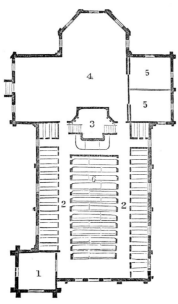

DESIGN LXXVI.

EPISCOPALIAN CHURCH.

THIS is a very neat and beautiful design, which would be suitable for an Episcopalian church.

It is drawn in plain elevation, and when viewed from the ground will be much shortened in height. The design is adapted for execution in brown or dark-colored stone; or the wall surface may be built of small, neatly-pointed rough stones, and the window-dressings, angles, etc., may be of hard stone, fairly worked.

The spire and the roof are intended to be covered with two tints of ornamental slates. In any locality this edifice would prove highly ornamental. The carriage-porch is very desirable for rural churches.

The ground plan provides for one hundred and twenty-four pews. On the right of the chancel, and with an entrance from both the chancel and south transept, is a library, which may be used to contain the books belonging to the rector and Sunday-school, and as a study. On the left of the chancel, with an entrance from the chancel and north transept, is a room for the accommodation of the vestry. The chancel is of ample size. Cost of construction, $30,000.

Description.—A, side entrance; B, vestibule; C, aisle; D, entrance-porch; E, nave; F, vestry; G, chancel; H, library; I, I, side aisles; J, north transept; K, south transept.

DESIGN LXXVI.

Episcopalian Church.

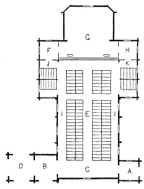

DESIGN LXXVII.

PLAIN FRENCH VILLA.

THIS plain French villa was built of bricks, painted. By the addition of dormers upon the tower, and a railing with a few telling lines, it can be made a beautiful house; and the ground plan is commodious, though needing some changes to render it first-class. The kitchen does not communicate with the dining-room, as we would desire; but as there are many valuable points in the design, we insert it. The cost of construction is $9000.

The height of the first floor is 12 feet; of the second, 11 feet; with good rooms above.

First Floor.—1, porch, 8 by 11 feet; 2, hall, 8 by 12 feet; 3, living-room, 15 by 25 feet; 4, sitting-room, 15 by 19 feet; 5, dining-room, 16 by 26 feet; 6, library, 12 by 15 feet; 7, porch, 6 feet; 8, kitchen, 22 by 13 feet; 9, china-closet, 6 by 6 feet; 10, scullery, 6 by 6 feet.

Second Floor.—15, 16, bed-rooms; 17, chamber, 12 by 15 feet; 18, chamber, 16 by 20 feet; 19, hall; 20, chamber, 15 by 21 feet; 21, chamber, 8 by 8 feet; 22, chamber, 15 by 19 feet; 23, balcony; 24, servants' stairs.

DESIGN LXXVII.

Plain French Villa.

FIRST FLOOR.

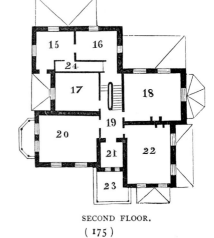

SECOND FLOOR.

(175)

DESIGN LXXVIII.

SUBURBAN RESIDENCE.

THIS design is in the Italian style, and will recommend itself. The accommodations are most ample; and the building has the latest improvements, being erected of rubble-work, pointed, with stone dressings to the windows and at the angles. The roof can be of tin. Upon the principal floor a projecting veranda gives access to main hall, parlor, sitting-room, dining-room, office and chamber, with a bath-room. The conservatory adjoins the parlor; and the butler's pantry, of sufficient size, adjoins the dining-room; the kitchen and wash-room are very conveniently arranged. The cost would be $30,000, being very large.

First Floor.—1, front porch; 2, grand hall, 14 feet; 3, parlor, 20 feet by 15 feet; 4, conservatory, 10 feet 6 inches by 12 feet; 5, sitting-room, 22 feet by 18 feet; 6, chamber, 16 feet by 18 feet; 7, bath-room, 8 feet 9 inches by 4 feet 6 inches; 8, office, 9 feet by 7 feet; 9, dining-room, 19 by 13 feet 11 inches; 10, butler's pantry, 6 feet by 6 feet 10 inches; 11, kitchen, 15 by 16 feet 11 inches; 12, wash-room, 10 feet 6 inches by 16 feet 11 inches; 13, closet; 14, back porch.

Second Floor.—15, veranda; 16, principal chamber, 20 feet by 15 feet; 17, dressing-room, 11 feet 10 inches by 16 feet; 18, bath-room, 8 feet by 6 feet 8 inches; 19, chamber, 16 feet by 18 feet; 20, chamber, 15 feet by 8 feet 9 inches; 21, chamber, 16 feet by 8 feet 7 inches; 22, closet; 23, chamber, 13 feet by 12 feet; 24, chamber, 13 feet by 14 feet; 25, closet, 3 feet by 7 feet; 26, closet, 3 feet by 7 feet; 27, chamber, 15 feet by 13 feet.

DESIGN LXXVIII.

Suburban Residence.

FIRST FLOOR.

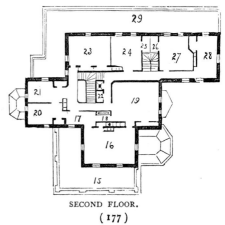

SECOND FLOOR.

(177)

DESIGN LXXIX.

COUNTRY RESIDENCE.

THE plan of this building was designed according to a ground plan by Mr. Huber, conveyancer, and is arranged with reference to economy and comfort. It contains fine halls in the first and second stories, with two comfortable rooms in the third story, and four rooms on the second and first stories, so arranged that they are placed conveniently with each other. It will make a roomy and cheap house, which would cost, if built of pointed-rubble masonry, in Philadelphia or vicinity, $7500.

The roof will be covered by ornamental-formed slates, with a flat tin roof on top, which answers as an observatory. Included in the estimate are the baths, water-closets, gas pipes throughout, low-down grates, marbelized-slate mantels in two rooms, sink, range, and a heater in the cellar; also, all modern improvements,—speaking-tubes, bells, etc.

First Floor.—1, front porch; 2, sitting-room, 15 by 18 feet; 3, hall, 7 feet; 4, parlor, 17 by 18 feet; 5, pantry, 6 by 8 feet 6 inches; 6, dining-room, 13 by 20 feet; 7, kitchen, 13 by 15 feet; 8, 9, closets.

Second Floor.—10, hall, 7 feet; 11, chamber, 15 by 18 feet; 12, chamber, 17 by 18 feet; 13, chamber, 13 by 20 feet; 14, chamber, 13 by 15 feet; 15, bath-room, 7 feet 6 inches by 8 feet 6 inches; 16, 17, 18, 19, closets.

DESIGN LXXIX.

Country Residence.

FIRST FLOOR.

SECOND FLOOR.

DESIGN LXXX.

ORNAMENTAL RESIDENCE.

THIS design is in the American style of architecture. All our buildings we aim to make light and airy. We continue to introduce turret-, bay-, and oriel-windows; and are not afraid to use whatever is beautiful, and in harmony with good taste and common sense. We would not decorate a pavilion with hanging men or beheaded women; neither would we embellish a dining-room with mummies, to carry out Egyptian or any other kind of architecture; nor would we place the most delicate of Grecian pediments in front of a jail or police station, skull-bones or buzzard-looking animals we consider more appropriate. This house will cost $10,000.

First Floor.—H, hall, 8 feet; L, library, 13 by 16 feet; P, dining-room, 25 by 16 feet; D, parlor, 22 by 16 feet; K, kitchen, 14 by 15 feet; P, P, porches.

Second Floor.—P C, principal chamber, 22 by 16 feet; C, chamber, 21 by 16 feet; C, chamber, 14 by 15 feet; C, chamber, 13 by 16 feet; D, hall; B R, bath-room, 8 by 5 feet 4 inches.

DESIGN LXXX.

Ornamental Residence.

FIRST FLOOR.

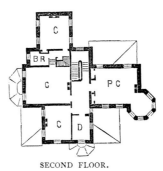

SECOND FLOOR.

DESIGN LXXXI.

GOTHIC SUBURBAN RESIDENCE.

THIS building was designed and built for Richard Brown, Esq., Youngstown, Ohio. It cost $33,000. The superstructure is of bricks, rubbed down, painted and sanded. The dressings, cornice, and base of house, is of cream-colored Ohio stone, finely cut, with rubbed heads. The interior is of a new style of finish, of our invention. The inside blinds are of "Hobbs' patent brass rod, double pivot." They are very superior, and capable of being cleaned,—having no rod in the centre,—which is a great improvement over the old process. The inside work is of fine quality,—walnut, rubbed down, French polish. The elevation is four feet high. First floor, 14 feet; second floor, 13 feet; with fine rooms on the third floor. The whole is well ventilated, and the roof of ornamental slates.

First Floor.—A, front and side porch; B, hall, 9 feet wide; C, parlor, 15 by 30 feet; D, sitting-room, 15 by 16 feet 9 inches; E, dining-room, 16 by 26 feet; F, kitchen, 13 by 20 feet; G, chamber, 14 feet 9 inches by 18 feet; H, bath-room, 8 feet 6 inches by 11 feet; vestibule, 7 by 9 feet.

Second Floor.—J, chamber, 15 by 30 feet; K, chamber, 15 by 16 feet 9 inches; L, chamber, 14 feet 9 inches by 18 feet; M, chamber, 16 by 26 feet; N, chamber, 13 by 20 feet; O, hall; S, dressing-room, 6 by 9 feet; P, bath-room, 8 feet 6 inches by 11 feet.

DESIGN LXXXI.

Gothic Suburban Residence.

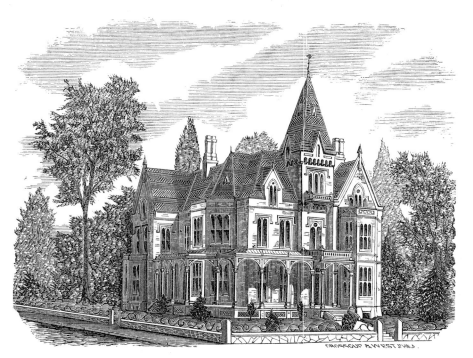

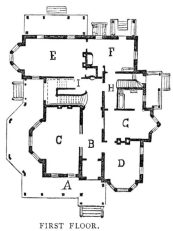

FIRST FLOOR.

SECOND FLOOR.

DESIGN LXXXII.

SOUTHERN COTTAGE.

THIS design is intended to be built of frame, and the roof to be shingled. It should stand at such a distance from the road as to afford sufficient space for ornamental shrubbery, walks, etc. The cost of the building should fall within the limits of four or five thousand dollars.

Upon the principal floor the porch gives access to the hall, which opens into the parlor and dining-room ; the kitchen is well placed, and ample in size. The second floor contains a hall and three liberal-sized chambers.

First Floor.—1, porch ; 2, hall, 10 feet 6 inches by 15 feet; 3, parlor, 12 feet 6 inches by 20 feet; 4, dining-room, 15 by 18 feet; 5, kitchen, 12 by 12 feet; 6, back porch.

Second Floor.—7, hall, 10 feet 6 inches by 15 feet; 8, chamber, 12 feet 6 inches by 20 feet; 9, chamber, 15 by 18 feet; 10, chamber, 12 by 12 feet.

DESIGN LXXXII.

Southern Cottage.

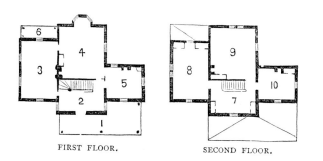

FIRST FLOOR. SECOND FLOOR.

DESIGN LXXXIII.

COUNTRY RESIDENCE.

THIS box-design by some means got among ours.
It is a fair example of designs published all over
the country. Its errors are as follows: the roof is
too low,—the dormer-windows ugly, and of a bad
shape; the top cornice is too heavy, and the main
cornice too light; the brackets are unsightly, and
wrong placed; the second-floor windows are good,
except their heads, which are coarse, and of no design; the porch is too low, and its posts too thin,
and its cornice of no account; the brackets upon it
are worse than none, and the lower windows are too
short; the bay is too small and meagre, and the back
building not decent for a carpenter's design. It has
no more design in it than a wood-shed ought to
have, and the perspective is not true. We publish it
subject to our criticism. It is set too low, and has no
cellar windows, or ventilation under porch; no chimneys on main roof that you can see; and it would
require ladders to look out of the dormer-windows
in the third floor. Such miserable, deceptive things
as this are published every year by the hundred, and
are the means of disappointment and waste of money,
besides exerting a corrupt influence. We could
without doubt make this design a very beautiful
building, by correcting its proportion, and giving
balance and weight to the whole; yet when so organized it would look as much like the picture as
a finely dressed person would to a shabby one.

DESIGN LXXXIII.
Country Residence.

FIRST FLOOR.

SECOND FLOOR.

DESIGN LXXXIV.

SUBURBAN RESIDENCE.

Ovo Gamber American design, of great economy in comparison to apparent size. It has a frontage of 56 feet. By examining the size and number of rooms it will be found not large or unwieldy; no wide rooms throughout. The front vestibule can be tiled; the hall and stairways are so located that they are handy and economical in situation. In executing this design, although much broken in appearance, all are of such form as to make no more work than square projections. The porch terminates against the house at each end, saving return cornice, etc. The whole can be constructed for between $6000 and $7000, fully supplied with the best quality heater, marble mantels, and gas throughout, cellar under the whole, and most thoroughly ventilated. The stories are 12 feet first floor, 11 second, and 10 the French roof. Numerous evolutions of this plan can be readily organized by us to suit locality, and also to be in harmony with surrounding buildings. It can be built of stone, brick, or wood, at pleasure. It suits a broad front lot, not exposed to rear view. If built as the plan shown, the design can be readily arranged to suit any situation and direction of view.

First Floor.—P, parlor, 16 by 22 feet 9 inches; S, sitting-room, 16 by 16 feet 9 inches; D, dining-room, 15 by 16 feet; K, kitchen, 11 feet 6 inches by 15 feet; O, hat-closet.

Second Floor.—E, store-room, 11 feet 6 inches by 5 feet; B, bath-room, 7 feet 3 inches by 10 feet 3 inches; C, chamber, 15 by 16 feet; C, chamber, 16 by 16 feet 9 inches; C, chamber, 16 by 22 feet 9 inches; F, sewing-room, 7 by 13 feet 6 inches.

DESIGN LXXXIV.

Suburban Residence.

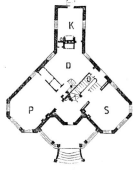

FIRST FLOOR.

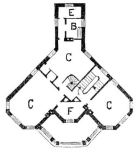

SECOND FLOOR.

DESIGN LXXXV.

SUBURBAN RESIDENCE.

THE above design is a plain, square house, but it is so constructed that the dining-room and kitchen have each a window looking to the front; their projections are dropped in the second story, which makes a less complicated roof. This building can be readily built for $4000, with the conveniences of gas, water, etc., introduced in the house. There is a fine cellar under the whole, built of bricks, hollow walls, 15 inches thick. A very compact and beautiful house for a village or suburban retreat, and can be placed upon a sixty-feet front lot.

We can organize any of these designs so that they will meet the wants of different persons, and arrange them without materially changing the appearance and character of the design; as musical notes, they can be in discord or harmonious, liquid or sharp. Character refers in design to the feeling that is produced by the predominance of lines, having within them certain fixed natural principles, co-ordinated with the human mind through the progress from youth to maturity; the smiles, frowns, or melancholy feelings are all shown by lines in the face, and they cast upon the beholder a corresponding thought.

First Floor.—P, parlor, 13 feet 8 inches by 20 feet; S R, sitting-room, 13 feet 8 inches by 13 feet 9 inches; B, chamber, 13 feet 8 inches by 12 feet; D, dining-room, 22 feet 3 inches by 13 feet 9 inches; K, kitchen, 13 feet 9 inches by 16 feet 8 inches.

Second Floor.—C, chamber, 13 feet 8 inches by 20 feet; C, chamber, 13 feet 8 inches by 13 feet 9 inches; C, chamber, 12 feet by 13 feet 8 inches; C, chamber, 13 feet 9 inches by 18 feet; R, bath-room, 8 feet 2 inches by 10 feet 4 inches; M, sewing-room, 8 feet 2 inches by 13 feet 9 inches; C L, china-closet; O, closets.

DESIGN LXXXV.

Suburban Residence.

FIRST FLOOR.

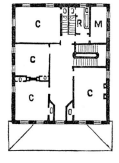

SECOND FLOOR.

DESIGN LXXXVI.

SUBURBAN RESIDENCE.

THIS design is a gabled cottage, French roof house, placed in company with pointed roofs, of cottage architecture; this will be in keeping, a too sudden change that often does take place in neighborhoods rendering buildings that would be beautiful look as though they were out of proportion. It is intended to be built of brick, rubbed down when laid, and then painted some appropriate stone-color. The roofs are of slate, cut ornamental pattern. It is a showy design; the plans are compact and handy, and all is well lighted; and can be built for $5000, first-class.

First Floor.—P, parlor, 15 feet 10 inches by 20 feet; L, library, 10 feet by 18 feet 6 inches; D R, dining-room, 15 by 15 feet; K, kitchen, 12 feet by 12 feet; H, hall; C C, china-closet, 5 feet 6 inches by 3 feet 6 inches; W C, water-closet.

Second Floor.—C, chamber, 15 by 20 feet; C, chamber, 10 by 14 feet; C, chamber, 15 by 15 feet; C, chamber, 12 by 8 feet 3 inches; O, closets; W C, water-closets; L C, linen-closets.

DESIGN LXXXVI.

Suburban Residence.

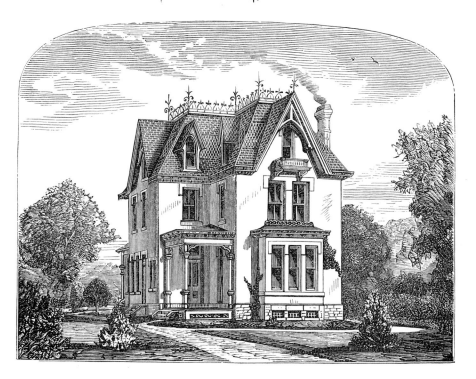

FIRST FLOOR.

SECOND FLOOR.

(193)

DESIGN LXXXVII.

SUBURBAN MANSION.

THIS design is an evolution of the Ovo laws of proportion, with a Mansard roof. It was erected for William M. Weigley, in Shafferstown, Lebanon County, Pennsylvania, of brown stone, from the quarry of Wm. M. Weigley. There is a ridge of brown stone running through his lands, of a peculiar rich reddish-brown color. The work was rock-face range work, with draughted base course, and other dressings of picked centres. The building was finely finished interiorly with hard natural wood. The situation of the house rendered it of an advantage to have a broad front, and not very deep. Much depends upon the lay and shape of the grounds, for the plan of a house to be effective, and original designs become necessary to successful operations. The building cost $22,000. The interior arrangements are as follows:

First Floor.—V, vestibule, 6 by 12 feet; H, stair-hall, 10 feet wide, connecting main hall 10 feet, separated by an ornamental arch connection; P, parlor, 15 feet wide by 30 feet long; L, library and sitting-room, 15 by 15 feet wide; an octagonal corner room, 10 feet in diameter, forming an alcove of beautiful proportions; A is a conservatory; D R, dining-room, 15 by 26 feet long; K, kitchen, 15 by 17 feet; S, scullery, 15 by 16 feet.

Second Floor contains four fine chambers, marked C, all of which are 15 feet wide and of the following lengths :—one with octagonal projecting tower alcove, 15 by 15 feet, alcove 10 feet; two 15 by 25 feet; one 15 by 17 feet 4 inches. This story also contains a dressing-room or boudoir, 11 by 13 feet; a bath-room, 10 by 11 feet, with ample linen and other closets.

DESIGN LXXXVII.

Suburban Mansion.

FIRST FLOOR.

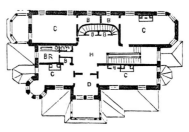

SECOND FLOOR.

DESIGN LXXXVIII.

AMERICAN COTTAGE VILLA.

Iᴛ is a good sample of modern buildings now being
built through the Southern States; it will cost to
construct, of frame, about $4000 to $5000; it has a
large frontage, and, suitably situated, will produce a
fine effect. All of these designs are organized to meet
the wants of our customers, and many times we are
even held by existing foundations. We are very
often furnished by ladies the general disposition of
halls, rooms, etc., so that we have merely to make
the same practical, so that they can be built, making
as few alterations as possible to obtain that result.
We rarely, if ever, fail to meet the full wants of families
by the adoption of such a course, and know of no
buildings failing to please the owner when built, except
the price is sometimes above their wants. When so,
we alter to suit them.

First Floor.—H, hall, 8 feet; P, parlor, 18 feet by 19
feet 6 inches; C, chamber, 16 by 16 feet; C, chamber,
14 by 18 feet; C, chamber, 14 by 18 feet; D-R, dining-
room, 16 by 18 feet; K, kitchen, 16 by 18 feet.

Second Floor.—C, chamber, 18 feet by 19 feet 6
inches; C, chamber, 14 by 18 feet; C, chamber, 14
by 18 feet; S R, sitting-room, 16 by 18 feet; B R,
bed-room, 16 by 18 feet.

DESIGN LXXXVIII.

American Cottage Villa.

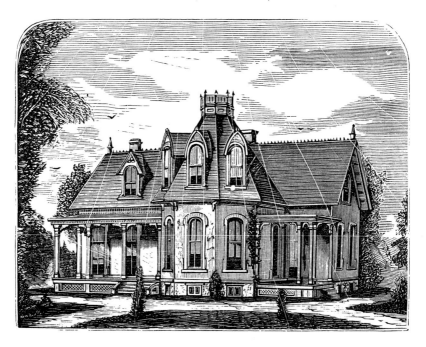

FIRST FLOOR.

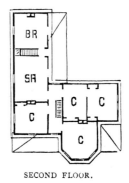

SECOND FLOOR.

DESIGN LXXXIX.

AMERICAN COTTAGE.

THIS design was drawn by us for the Rev. John D. McClintock, Huntingdon, West Va. It is one of those American cottages containing very liberal accommodations for a small family. Its cost, finely finished, of bricks, painted neat, with porches and well-finished interior, was $3446.25 ; built of frame, would cost $3000. It is slated with slates from the True Blue Quarry, Pennsylvania. These slates come very regular in color, are durable and strong; ornamentally laid, they cost 12 cents per square foot. The hall and parlor are finished in chestnut and other natural woods, oiled and rubbed down. Care has been taken with the proportions. The windows are large, and the interior is finished with heaters, slate mantels, and range complete for this sum. Such buildings are needed, and we design numbers of them for various persons all over the country. They sell at good price and give universal satisfaction. Every situation demands different treatment, and the arrangements of the rooms can be suited to any locality and the taste of the owner.

First Floor.—P, parlor, 15 by 16 feet; F R, family-room, 15 by 16 feet; O, office, 15 by 16 feet; D R, dining-room, 12 by 14 feet; K, kitchen, 10 by 11 feet; B R, bath-room, 6 by 7 feet; P, pantry; H, hall, 6 feet.

Second Floor.—C, chamber, 15 by 16 feet; C, chamber, 15 by 16 feet.

DESIGN LXXXIX.

American Cottage.

FIRST FLOOR.

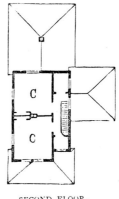

SECOND FLOOR.

(199)

DESIGN XC.

AMERICAN SUBURBAN RESIDENCE.

THIS design was erected from our drawing, by William P. Debott, Union county, Indiana. It has a sandstone base, with window-sills and heads of the same material. The superstructure is of bricks, shingle roof, covered with fire-proof paint, and its cost when fully finished was about $8000. We are constantly making for parties designs similar to the above, with varied evolutions, interior and external, in various parts of the United States, no two of which are ever precisely alike. Persons ordering such houses should be very careful to have every part fully understood before commencing, and any thing short of full drawings will be found dangerous and expensive.

First Floor.—P, parlor, 16 by 23 feet; S R, sitting-room, 15 by 16 feet; L, library, 14 by 14 feet; D R, dining-room, 15 by 19 feet; C, chamber, 12 by 14 feet; K, kitchen, 14 by 16 feet; S, scullery, 11 by 14 feet.

Second Floor.—P C, principal chamber, 16 by 23 feet; C, chamber over sitting-room, 15 by 16 feet; C, chamber over dining-room, 15 by 19 feet; C, chamber over library, 14 by 14 feet; C, chamber over chamber, 12 by 14 feet.

DESIGN XC.

American Suburban Residence.

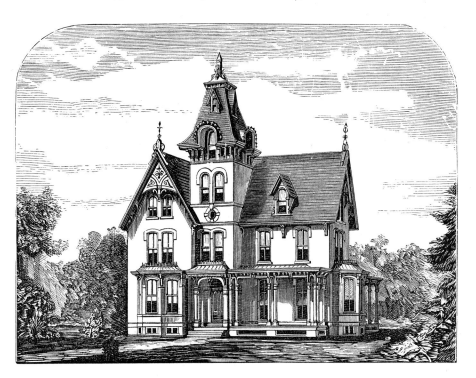

FIRST FLOOR.

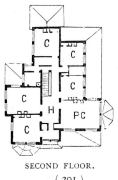

SECOND FLOOR.

(201)

DESIGN XCI.

SUBURBAN RESIDENCE.

THIS design was built for John W. Stoddard, Esq., on a very commanding situation overlooking the city of Dayton, Ohio. The base of the building, as high as the first floor, is of white limestone; the trimmings around the windows, doors, cornices, etc., are of Ohio sandstone, finely cut and rubbed. The roof is slate, the top of flat roof is tin. In the erection of the building no pains were spared to render it one of the finest finished residences of the city. The superstructure is of brick, laid flush joints, and rubbed down for painting. By a reference to the plans, it will be found compact and commodious; it is finished inside with black and white walnut. The richness of this latter wood is peculiarly fine around Dayton. The grain is capable of being matched in fine figures; it is of a lighter color than the other walnut, darker than chestnut, and when rubbed down in oil polish its effects are fine. It will cost $25,000.

We are willing to contrast it for beauty or elegance of effect, or costly appearance, with any other building in the vicinity.

First Floor.—P, parlor, 16 by 26 feet; S R, sitting-room, 16 by 20 feet; R P, reception parlor, 12 feet 6 inches by 16 feet; D R, dining-room, 15 by 20 feet 10 inches; B R, breakfast-room, 12 by 13 feet; K, kitchen, 16 by 16 feet 3 inches; L, lavatory, 4 feet 8 inches by 7 feet 6 inches; V, vestibule, 6 by 11 feet 3 inches; H, hall; C, china-closet; C C, closets.

DESIGN XCI.

Suburban Residence.

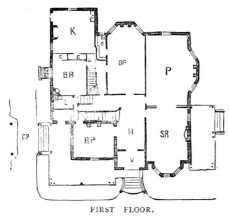

FIRST FLOOR.

DESIGN XCII.

AN AMERICAN COTTAGE.

THIS design is of a Franco-American cottage. It is one of those kind of designs possible with any person building a home, and desiring the conveniences and capacity afforded here. It can be built upon a fifty-feet front lot, and not crowd the grounds, is capable of being set back some distance from the front of the lot, and could be placed to good effect from sixteen to thirty-five feet back. The French roof is so constructed that a sufficient loft of attic will be above the second-story rooms, which, by the system of ventilation we adopt, renders them cool and comfortable in summer. French roofs require architectural proportions more than any other structure we know of. Hence the reason of thousands of failures in this style of architecture; but if properly proportioned they are very beautiful.

First Floor.—H, hall; P, parlor, 14 feet 6 inches by 15 feet 6 inches; L R, living-room, 14 feet 6 inches by 17 feet; B R, bed-room, 7 feet 6 inches by 15 feet; D R, dining-room, 13 by 16 feet; K, kitchen, 13 by 13 feet.

Second Floor.—C, chamber, 14 feet 6 inches by 16 feet; C, chamber, 14 feet 6 inches by 17 feet; C, chamber, 13 by 16 feet; B R, bed-room, 13 by 13 feet; B R, bath-room, 7 feet 6 inches by 11 feet.

DESIGN XCII.

An American Cottage.

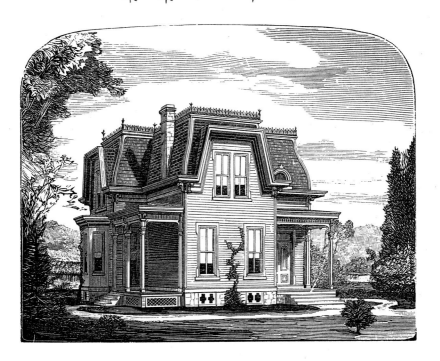

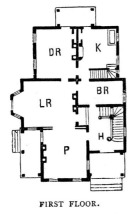

FIRST FLOOR.

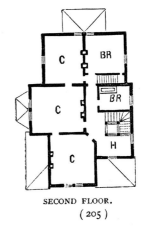

SECOND FLOOR.

(205)

DESIGN XCIII.

SUBURBAN RESIDENCE.

This suburban residence was built, under our superintendence, upon a very commanding site upon the heights north of the Falls of the Schuylkill, Philadelphia, upon ten acres of ground. The building overlooks the Park, and can be seen from almost all the drives to Germantown and Falls of Schuylkill, and many drives in the Park. It was built for James Dobson, Esq., an extensive manufacturer of this city. The superstructure is built of Falls of Schuylkill stone, laid rubble and pointed with white mortar; the roof is of slates. By reference to the plans, it will be observed that it is very commodious inside, and is finished in the most elaborate manner with black walnut, finely polished, throughout the first and second floors. The building has fine porch accommodations, a conservatory, and all modern improvements, to render it one of the most complete rural residences about the city. Its cost was about $40,000 when completed in every part. We have also erected upon the plantation a fine, commodious carriage-house, in keeping with the architecture of the house. It is built by the Ovo law of proportion, and we consider it a successful example.

First Floor.—V, vestibule, 7 feet 6 inches by 12 feet; H, hall, 12 feet wide; P, parlor, 17 by 55 feet; C, conservatory, 13 by 17 feet; L, library, 17 by 20 feet; D R, dining-room, 16 feet 6 inches by 26 feet; K, kitchen, 14 feet 6 inches by 17 feet 6 inches; S, scullery, 11 feet by 17 feet 6 inches.

Second Floor.—H, hall, 12 feet wide; P C, principal chamber, 17 feet by 36 feet 6 inches; C, chamber, 17 by 18 feet; C, chamber, 17 by 18 feet; C, chamber, 16 feet 6 inches by 26 feet; B, bath-room, 11 by 12 feet; C, chamber, 14 by 15 feet; C, chamber, 10 feet 6 inches by 11 feet 6 inches.

DESIGN XCIII.

Suburban Residence

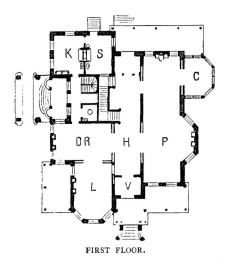

FIRST FLOOR.

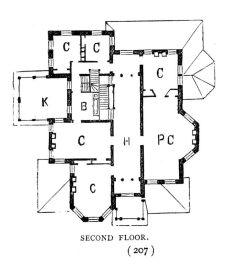

SECOND FLOOR.

(207)

DESIGN XCIV.

AMERICAN ORNAMENTAL VILLA.

THIS ornamental villa was designed for and built by A. D. Gyger, Esq., at Bird-in-Hand, a station on the Pennsylvania Railroad, about six miles east of Lancaster. It has given great satisfaction, both in appearance externally and inside arrangements. It is commodious, free, and capable of being furnished with elegance. The windows are fitted with our patent blinds, and the architraves are of a new design, used extensively by our firm. The heavy part is placed next to the door or window, and the wash-board moulding sweeps around them by having a small ring turned of their shape, and cut in four quarters, each quarter being placed in the corners of each top, and one on the bottom, so that by an easy sweep the mouldings pass from the wash-board around the door.

This building is of brick, laid flush, joints rubbed down, and painted. Its cost was about $20,000 with all conveniences. We have recently invented a new mode of making sash requiring no putty, also a window-frame, with an improved pulley-stile, requiring no parting-strips or sash-beads; the pulleys and sash-cords are hidden from view. The sash can be taken out and placed back without disfiguring the paint.

First Floor.—V, vestibule, 7 feet 3 inches by 7 feet 3 inches; P, parlor, 20 feet by 27 feet 10 inches; L, library, 14 by 14 feet; D R, dining-room, 14 by 22 feet; K, kitchen, 15 by 17 feet; S R, store-room, 4 feet 3 inches by 10 feet; S, scullery, 10 feet by 11 feet 6 inches; H, hall, 8 feet wide.

Second Floor.—D R, dressing-room, 7 feet 3 inches by 10 feet 9 inches; P C, principal chamber, 20 feet by 27 feet 10 inches; C, chamber, 14 by 15 feet 3 inches; C, chamber, 12 feet 9 inches by 18 feet 9 inches; C, chamber, 15 by 17 feet, with a bath-room 5 feet by 10 feet 4 inches.

DESIGN XCIV.

American Ornamental Villa.

FIRST FLOOR.

SECOND FLOOR.

(209)

DESIGN XCV.

AN AMERICAN COTTAGE.

THIS design is a beautiful type of an American home. We have many orders for drawings of such styles of houses. Some people persist in filling their houses with closets, and, when in excess, they become hiding-places. There should be a commodious closet and clothes-press in every chamber. The kitchen should have ample places for its necessary articles; the store-room, butler's pantry, are all needed. This building can be built for $2500 very complete, by good superintendence on the part of the owner in purchasing materials, and seeing that they are used economically. The house is of frame, covered with felt and weather-boarding; this felt is now manufactured quite thick, and nailed upon the studding. The roof may be shingles or slate; there is an air-space or loft above the second floor. An open communication from below the cornice must be made to communicate with it all around, and there must be two flues, one open at the bottom of this loft, and passing through the roof, and the other open at the top of loft, and opening out high above. This insures a constant change of air in the vault, and renders the upper rooms cool and comfortable at all times.

First Floor.—H, hall, 10 feet wide; P, parlor, 16 by 22 feet; S R, sitting-room, 16 by 18 feet; D R, dining-room, 14 by 22 feet; C, chamber, 14 by 18 feet; K, kitchen, 14 by 18 feet.

Second Floor.—C, chamber, 16 by 22 feet; C, chamber, 10 by 10 feet; C, chamber, 16 by 18 feet; C, chamber, 14 by 18 feet; C, chamber, 14 by 22 feet; C, chamber, 14 by 18 feet.

DESIGN XCV.

An American Cottage.

FIRST FLOOR.

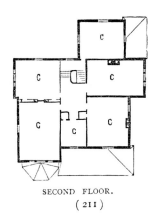

SECOND FLOOR.

DESIGN XCVI.

MODEL RESIDENCE.

THIS building was designed for P. K. Boyd, Esq., of Harrisburg, Pennsylvania, and is built opposite the front entrance of the State Capitol.

The base of the building and the window and door dressings are of Berea stone, from Ohio, and the superstructure is of brick; the porches, cornices, etc., are of wood, with the roof of slates and tin. The interior is finely finished in polished walnut. The inside shutters and finish are of Hobbs's improved style, giving massive and artistic effect upon entering. The house is very commodious and supplied with all the new improvements, at a cost of about $20,000. It was built under a system of giving each mechanic an opportunity to estimate for his own work, making the brick-layer, carpenter, and plasterer, etc., each responsible to the owner, and also supplying each branch of mechanics with an opportunity of receiving the merit of his particular branch of work,—a mode which is rapidly gaining favor. It insures the owner against liens, by having every cent paid, and saves all the trouble and vexation in obtaining releases, as all who have had contract work done can appreciate.

First Floor—V, vestibule, 6 by 8 feet; H, hall, 8 feet wide; P, parlor, 15 by 30 feet; L, library, 15 by 26 feet 5 inches; D R, dining-room, 15 by 24 feet; K, kitchen, 13 feet 9 inches by 18 feet 4 inches; C, china-closet, 5 feet 2 inches by 8 feet 6 inches; P, pantry, 5 feet 2 inches by 8 feet 6 inches.

Second Floor.—D, dressing-room, 8 feet by 9 feet 6 inches; C, chamber, 15 feet 4 inches by 23 feet 8 inches; C, chamber, 15 feet 4 inches by 23 feet 1 inch; B, bath-room, 6 by 10 feet 2 inches; C, chamber, 15 by 24 feet; C, chamber, 10 feet 5 inches by 24 feet.

DESIGN XCVI.

Model Residence.

FIRST FLOOR.

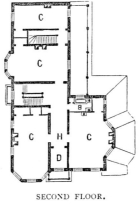

SECOND FLOOR.

(213)

DESIGN XCVII.

RURAL MODEL RESIDENCE.

THIS design was drawn and built for Mr. O. S. Hubbel, the well-known druggist of this city, at Rivercliffe, near Norwalk, Connecticut. He is the owner of the celebrated bird Ariel, the carrier-pigeon that has taken the premium as the best bird in the world. This building has met with his entire approbation, and he stated to us, that all who see it do not differ from the *Daily Graphic's* account of it as the handsomest house in the United States, of equal cost. It is plain and beautiful, and cost about $15,000 with interior well finished. We have recently made an invention of an entirely new style of finish for the inside of a house, that possesses the advantage of enabling persons to use walnut and other hard woods in the entire finish, with comparatively little or no addition in the cost over painted wood-work of the best quality white pine. We give our patrons the advantages of our invention. Those who are building under other architects, desiring to save money, obtain rich and beautiful apartments, can be supplied with details and drawings of the same at the rate of one per cent. upon the cost as per agreement.

First Floor.—H, hall, 8 feet wide; P, parlor, 16 by 16 feet; L, library, 12 by 20 feet; D R, dining-room, 16 by 16 feet; D R, drawing-room, 16 by 16 feet; K, kitchen, 13 by 19 feet 9 inches, with a larder 8 by 10 feet, and a store-closet 5 feet 6 inches by 8 feet 3 inches.

Second Floor.—C, chamber, 16 by 16 feet; C, chamber, 8 feet 4 inches by 12 feet; C, chamber, 16 by 16 feet; C, chamber, 12 feet 6 inches by 12 feet 6 inches; B R, bath-room, 5 feet 6 inches by 16 feet; D R, dressing-room, 5 by 8 feet 6 inches; C, chamber, 15 by 16 feet; C, chamber, 13 by 16 feet; D R, dressing-room, 5 by 8 feet, with a linen-closet 5 feet 6 inches by 7 feet.

DESIGN XCVII.

Rural Model Residence.

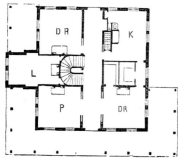

FIRST FLOOR.

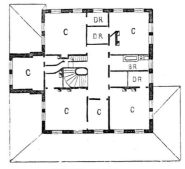

SECOND FLOOR.

DESIGN XCVIII.

ORNAMENTAL COTTAGE.

THIS design is an organization between the French and cottage style of treatment. It can be built for $6000 in frame, and in brick for $7000, the second story almost containing a full perpendicular one, a small angular slope near the ceiling caused by the roof, which makes a very fine internal effect. The roof is of slate, with the top of tin.

These designs are all original, and well considered. We are making great improvements in internal finish in houses, that renders them more beautiful and cheaper. We finish most of them without stucco cornices, plain straight walls, which are painted one coat with oil and white lead, and two coats of oil and turpentine, the third and fourth coat with encaustic varnish, tinted to any desired color. This encaustic varnish costs $2.50 per gallon, and two gallons will paint a parlor two coats, 15 by 30 feet, walls and ceilings. It becomes very hard and can be washed. Any turpentine, or other material, will cause lead to turn yellow in a darkened room with great rapidity, and you of necessity must use French zinc, which has not the solidity or durability of the best lead, and if pure is very expensive, and so the imitation article is resorted to. This mode of finish makes the ceilings look higher than they do with plaster cornices.

First Floor.—H, hall, 7 feet 6 inches wide; P, parlor, 15 by 17 feet 6 inches; S R, sitting-room, 12 by 15 feet; D R, dining-room, 13 by 14 feet; C, chamber, 9 by 15 feet; K, kitchen, 10 by 13 feet; L, library, 9 by 13 feet.

Second Floor.—H, hall; C, chamber, 14 feet 6 inches by 15 feet 6 inches; C, chamber, 11 feet 6 inches by 15 feet; C, chamber, 10 by 15 feet, with a large number of closets.

DESIGN XCVIII.

Ornamental Residence.

FIRST FLOOR.

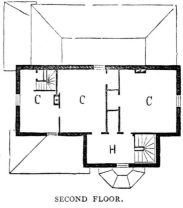

SECOND FLOOR.

(217)

DESIGN XCIX.

STRUCTURAL PARK RESIDENCE.

THIS design is a cheap Park residence of simple character. The kitchen wing is one story high. The house has four rooms on the first floor, three on the second, and three on the third. The stories are eleven, ten, and nine feet respectively, built in good style. Its cost of frame, weather-boarded, was $3000, and of bricks, painted, $3500. Persons approving of this style of architecture cannot fail to like this sample, as its proportions are well adjusted.

First Floor.—H, hall, 8 feet wide; P, parlor, 12 by 16 feet; D R, dining-room, 15 by 16 feet; L, library, 15 by 15 feet; K, kitchen, 15 by 16 feet.

Second Floor.—C, chamber, 12 by 16 feet; C, chamber, 15 by 15 feet; C, chamber, 10 by 16 feet; H, hall; and a number of closets.

DESIGN XCIX.

Structural Park Residence.

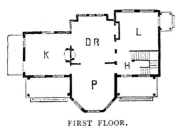

FIRST FLOOR.

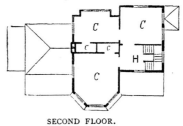

SECOND FLOOR.

DESIGN C.

PARK PICTURESQUE VILLA.

This design is intended as a country house. Its detail parts are simple and direct. It is not the kind of a house to build in prim uniform lines, as is common in villages. It will harmonize well with natural scenery, and can be constructed of frame, weather-boarded, at a cost of about $4000.

It has four fine porches, but no mouldings must be used in the design. The roof is covered with iron or tin. As we are continually receiving letters from persons who have attempted to build without an architect, and often those who have no experience get into difficulty, sometimes placing the house too high, at others too low, we will state to those persons that we are willing, at all times, to give them the advantages of our experience for a small fee, and it is rarely ever impossible to remedy the evil to a great extent.

Many hundreds of houses are spoiled by the painter alone, and we always advise to paint a house of one simple color, avoiding the color of dust and dirt of the vicinity, but if of the same tone it must be brighter, and have a cleanlier appearance.

First Floor.—H, hall; P, parlor, 12 by 14 feet 6 inches; D R, dining-room, 11 by 12 feet; K, kitchen, 12 by 12 feet; S, sink-room, 4 by 6 feet; C, conservatory, 7 by 12 feet; and a store-room, 4 by 6 feet.

Second Floor.—H, hall; P C, principal chamber, 12 by 14 feet; C, chamber, 11 by 12 feet; B, bed-room, 6 by 9 feet; B, bed-room, 6 by 9 feet; C C, closets.

DESIGN C.

Park Picturesque Villa.

FIRST FLOOR.

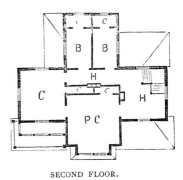

SECOND FLOOR.

DESIGN CI.

AMERICAN SUBURBAN RESIDENCE.

THIS design was drawn and designed by us for George M. Hambright, Esq., of Lancaster, Pa., and has four rooms on the first floor, four chambers on the second, and four on the third floor. The building can readily be placed upon a fifty-feet front lot. The proportions are good, and conveniently arranged. The house can be built of bricks, for $6000, and of frame, for $5000. It will be found to contain elegance and convenience, adaptable to many situations.

First Floor.—H, hall, 6 feet wide; P, parlor, 13 by 21 feet 6 inches; S, sitting-room, 12 by 12 feet 6 inches, with a bay-window 4 feet 6 inches by 9 feet; D R, dining-room, 13 by 17 feet; K, kitchen, 11 by 12 feet.

Second Floor.—C, chamber, 13 by 21 feet 6 inches; C, chamber, 12 by 12 feet; C, chamber, 13 by 17 feet; B, bed-room, 11 by 12 feet.

DESIGN CI.

American Suburban Residence.

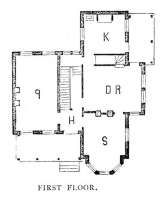

FIRST FLOOR.

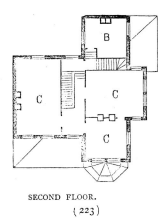

SECOND FLOOR.

(223)

DESIGN CII.

SUBURBAN RESIDENCE.

THIS suburban residence was drawn for B. C. Taylor, Esq., of the B. C. Taylor Manufacturing Company, of Dayton, Ohio, and is built on one of the fine avenues of that beautiful city. It is constructed of brick, with Berea stone trimmings, and contains all the modern improvements, viz., our new style of finish, a vast improvement over the old style. This new style of moulding entirely reverses the old method; the heavy side is next the door, and the wash-board moulding is located around them; also Hobbs's double-pivot blinds, which do away with the clumsy stick down the centre by the substitution of a silver-plated strip alongside of the stiles. They are adjustable up and down, and close perfectly tight, and are not moved by the wind. Care and new invention is brought to bear in every part of this structure. Its whole cost did not exceed $20,000, elegantly finished with butternut wood rubbed down in oil.

First Floor.—V, vestibule, 6 feet by 7 feet 6 inches; H, hall, 7 feet 6 inches wide; P, parlor, 15 by 20 feet; S R, sitting-rooms, 14 by 14 feet 6 inches; D R, dining-room, 14 feet 6 inches by 16 feet 3 inches; B R, bath-room, 5 feet 6 inches by 8 feet 6 inches; C, chamber, 10 feet 6 inches by 14 feet 6 inches; K, kitchen, 15 feet 8 inches by 17 feet; P R, pump-room, 7 by 7 feet; a pantry, 5 feet 6 inches by 11 feet 6 inches; and a large number of closets.

Second Floor.—C, chamber, 15 by 20 feet; C, chamber, 13 feet 6 inches by 14 feet; C, chamber, 13 feet 9 inches by 14 feet; C, chamber, 14 by 14 feet 6 inches; B R, bath-room, 5 feet 6 inches by 8 feet 6 inches; C, chamber, 10 feet 6 inches by 14 feet 6 inches; S R, bed-rooms, 10 by 14 feet; and a dressing-room, 7 feet 6 inches by 7 feet 6 inches.

DESIGN CII.

Suburban Residence.

FIRST FLOOR.

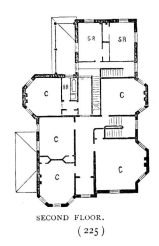

SECOND FLOOR.

(225)

DESIGN CIII.

FRENCH SUBURBAN RESIDENCE.

THIS design is a cheap French suburban residence. The interior is well arranged for comfort and convenience, and can be built in the vicinity of Philadelphia for $4000. Everywhere, in the United States and Canada, residents are availing themselves of our services. Any person ordering drawings for a house should always fully describe the location and size of the lot, the distance back from the road, width of its front, and the kind of building that will be in association with it, also, the grade of the grounds. We know this is troublesome, but it will be found to pay. When grounds are to be placed in artistic association, we must have the grades marked distinctly, and a map sent to us showing the plantation, which can always be executed by a surveyor. This saves money in grading and forming the same into fine effect, as many persons have fine plantations requiring but little to render them truly picturesque, with very little outlay, yet for want of practical knowledge, only obtained by experience and culture, they fail to obtain the same, and often destroy what would be their greatest beauty.

First Floor.—H, hall, 8 feet wide; P, parlor, 12 by 16 feet; D R, dining-room, 12 by 18 feet; K, kitchen, 12 by 16 feet; S, shed, 8 by 12 feet; C, conservatory.

Second Floor.—C, chamber, 12 by 16 feet; C, chamber, 12 by 18 feet; C, chamber, 10 by 16 feet; H, hall.

DESIGN CIII.

French Suburban Residence.

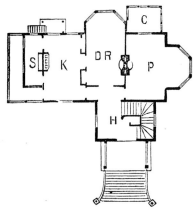

FIRST FLOOR.

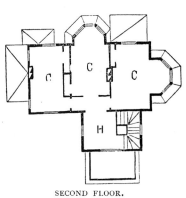

SECOND FLOOR.

(227)

DESIGN CIV.

SUBURBAN RESIDENCE.

THIS is a design of a Gothic villa, Americanized. It contains all the requisites of a first-class home. As a suburban residence, or country mansion, it has a refined, dignified, and substantial appearance, the plan having all the nobleness of the effect required. The parlor is commodious and elegant, of the finest decorations, and lighted, as it is, by bay-windows, the light will be thrown upon the walls, that paintings and statuary may have full effect. By the use of sliding doors, the main hall becomes a part of the parlor. It is intended to have a dumb-waiter in the rear, so as to render the kitchen apartment perfect, as they are in the rear of the house and in basement. The slope of the grounds at the back of the building affords fine ventilation and light.

First Floor.—A, porch; P, parlor, 19 by 29 feet; L, library, 15 by 17 feet; H, hall, 10 feet wide; S H, stair-hall; D, dining-room, 15 by 24 feet 6 inches; S, sitting-room, 15 by 15 feet; C P, carriage-porch.

Second Floor.—D R, dressing-room, 10 by 13 feet; P C, principal chamber, 16 by 25 feet; C, chamber, 15 by 15 feet; H, hall; A, conservatory; C, chamber, 15 feet by 24 feet 6 inches; C, chamber, 15 by 15 feet.

DESIGN CIV.

Suburban Residence.

FIRST FLOOR.

SECOND FLOOR.

DESIGN CV.

MODEL RESIDENCE.

THIS design is in the Ovo order of architecture. There is nothing guessed at in its proportions, but all is evolved in a positive law regulating the whole. All of the members, brackets, and cornices, have a relative character of parts, as well as a decided quantity of plain to ornamental surface. The building was designed for and built by Mr. Garrettson, of Pottsville, at a cost of $18,000. It has given great satisfaction, and is very ornamental. The interior is well arranged to suit a peculiar situation, standing on a wall at its rear that separates the lot from the railroad, of some twenty feet high, the principal street being at an elevation of thirty feet above. The lot being shallow, every inch of room had to be arranged in the most economical manner, and we say it is a great success. The first story is twelve feet, the second, eleven feet, third, eleven feet high.

First Floor.—A, porch; V, vestibule, 6 by 8 feet; P, parlor, 16 by 23 feet; L, library, 16 by 9 feet; I, hall; S R, sitting-room, 16 by 19 feet; D R, dining-room, 21 by 26 feet; K, kitchen, 16 by 20 feet; S, scullery, 16 by 8 feet; C, conservatory: C H, carriage-house; H R, harness-room.

DESIGN CV.

Model Residence.

FIRST FLOOR.

DESIGN CVI.

MODEL RESIDENCE.

THIS design was drawn for and built by Mrs. Eshleman. It is situated on Duke street, Lancaster, Pa., and has given entire satisfaction. It is the most attractive house in the city, and has a carriage-house in the rear which is in good character with the dwelling. The house and dwelling cost about $24,000, with finely laid-out grounds. The house is painted in imitation of the Berea stone, of Ohio, with no change of color between the cornices and walls; when such change is made, in almost all cases it is done in a vulgar manner, and destroys the rays of light that good proportion throws upon the surface, when not marred by discordant colors. No one is willing to put a brown-stone cornice upon a white marble building, for the taste of all would decide for a white marble cornice to a marble house. The garden in front is all grass and walks, except flowers placed in vases. The stories of the house are twelve feet first story, eleven feet second, and twelve feet third or French roof.

First Floor.—V, vestibule, 6 by 8 feet wide; H, hall, 8 feet wide; P, parlor, 29 by 19 feet; L, library, 15 by 31 feet; D R, dining-room, 14 by 21 feet; K, kitchen, 12 by 17 feet.

Second Floor.—H, hall, 8 feet; P C, principal chamber, 19 by 23 feet; C, chamber, 15 by 15 feet; C, chamber, 12 by 15 feet; C, chamber, 14 by 17 feet; C, chamber, 12 by 21 feet 6 inches.

DESIGN CVI.

Model Residence.

FIRST FLOOR.

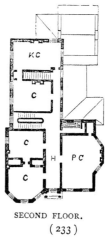

SECOND FLOOR.

DESIGN CVII.

THIS design in the American-Gothic style was built for Wm. M. Loyd, banker, at Altoona, Pa., a flourishing town on the line of the Central Railroad. The building is well situated, with a large plantation upon a sloping hill, the lawn in the front of the house being nearly six hundred feet, and when built it was one of princely effect. It is finished in black walnut in the finest style. The elevation is of pointed rubble masonry of mountain freestone, of a light color. The dressings are of Berea stone, of Ohio. Its cost was between $35,000 and $40,000. We have many other buildings in Altoona, as well as many of the other towns along the line of this road.

First Floor.—V, vestibule, 5 feet 4 inches by 10 feet; L, library, 12 by 14 feet 6 inches; P, parlor, 15 feet by 26 feet 6 inches; D R, dining-room, 15 by 19 feet; C, conservatory, 8 feet 6 inches by 10 feet 6 inches; P, pantry, 6 feet by 10 feet 6 inches; L, lavatory, 4 feet 6 inches by 6 feet 4 inches; K, kitchen, 14 by 14 feet; S R, store-room, 3 feet 9 inches by 10 feet 2 inches; S, scullery, 15 feet by 11 feet 6 inches; H, hall, 10 feet wide.

Second Floor.—D R, dressing-room, 7 feet 3 inches by 10 feet 4 inches; C, chamber, 12 feet 4 inches by 14 feet 6 inches; C, chamber, 15 feet by 20 feet 10 inches; C, chamber, 15 feet 7 inches by 17 feet 8 inches; B R, bath-room, 7 feet 4 inches by 10 feet; D R, dressing-room, 5 feet 3 inches by 9 feet 7 inches; C, chamber, 9 by 12 feet; C, chamber, 8 feet by 11 feet 7 inches; C, closets.

DESIGN CVII.

Model Residence.

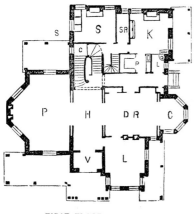

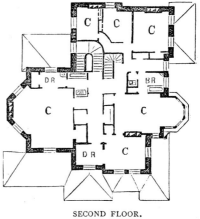

FIRST FLOOR.

SECOND FLOOR.

DESIGN CVIII.

SUBURBAN RESIDENCE.

THIS design was drawn to be built in Norwalk, Conn., where a number of our designs have been erected. This is drawn in simple elevation, a plain geometrical drawing supposing a person had a thousand eyes, and looking direct upon each separate part.

Persons can obtain no real information by this how the building will look when viewed perspectively. This is the process by which almost all architects get up their designs, which when finished often prove great failures. To design right we design in perspective, where the proportion, slopes of roof, height and size of objects are changed to the person viewing. The geometrical drawings are with us merely modes whereby the workman can have a guide and scale to get out his work from. As a rule this truth must be acknowledged, that if a line or geometrical drawing is beautiful, the structure when built will be ugly and all out of proportion, and without feeling, as they are not what they appear to be.

First Floor.—A, vestibule; B, hall, 10 feet wide; C, parlor, 16 by 30 feet; D, library, 15 by 18 feet; E, dining-room, 16 by 21 feet; G, china-closet; H, pantry; I, kitchen, 14 by 16 feet; J, scullery, 11 by 16 feet; K, carriage-porch; L, front porch.

Second Floor.—M, chambers; N, dressing-room; O, hall; P, bath-room.

DESIGN CVIII.

Suburban Residence.

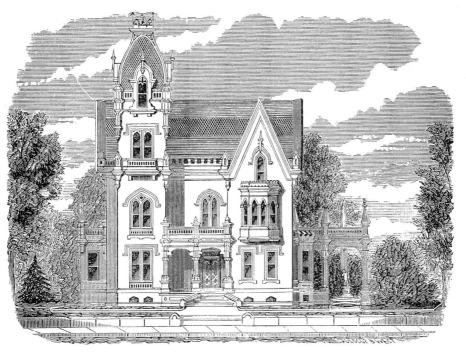

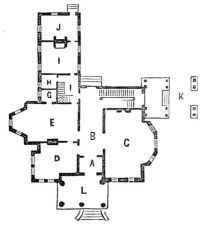

FIRST FLOOR.

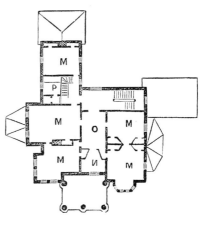

SECOND FLOOR.

(237)

DESIGN CIX.

SUBURBAN RESIDENCE.

THIS suburban residence is in the Franco-Italian style of architecture. Its proportions are extracted by the Ovo law of proportion, a law governing forms, character, and quantity. From a knowledge of the law above alluded to, there is a possibility of evolving combinations infinite in number, and beautiful in their type. We have always contended that beauty is not necessarily attendant upon high ornamentation or costly combinations, as we see many large and costly buildings entirely destitute of it, and many others, very simple, possessing it to a great degree.

First Floor.—V, vestibule ; H, hall, 12 feet wide ; P, parlor, 15 by 20 feet ; D R, drawing-room, 15 by 20 feet ; D R, dining-room, 15 by 25 feet ; K, kitchen, 10 by 18 feet ; S, study, 8 feet by 12 feet 6 inches ; C, conservatory.

Second Floor.—C, chamber, 15 by 20 feet ; C, chamber, 15 by 20 feet ; C, chamber, 15 by 20 feet ; D R, dressing-room, 8 by 10 feet ; B R, bath-room.

DESIGN CIX.

Suburban Residence.

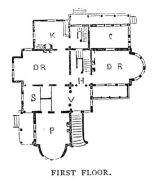

FIRST FLOOR.

SECOND FLOOR.

(239)

DESIGN CX.

FRENCH SUBURBAN RESIDENCE.

THIS design is made to meet the wants of a large number of persons wishing to construct a small residence of taste. This design can be readily built for between $4000 and $5000, different localities making considerable difference in their cost. It is intended to be built of frame, weather-boarded. The steep roof of ornamental cut slates, in two patterns, square and angular. It is best to cover the whole frame and roof with felt before putting on the weather-boards and slate roof, as it secures a warm and comfortable house. By reference to the plans, it will be observed to contain comfortable and free rooms. They are of sizes that render them beautiful. A number of these houses, situated upon some avenue in a town, would create a beautiful neighborhood. The first story is twelve feet high, the second and third, eleven feet in the clear.

First Floor.—A, porch; P, parlor, 12 by 15 feet; D, dining-room, 12 by 22 feet 8 inches; K, kitchen, 12 by 12 feet; S, scullery, 10 by 12 feet.

Second Floor.—P C, principal chamber, 12 by 15 feet; H, hall; C, C, chambers, 11 feet 4 inches by 12 feet; B P, bath-room, 7 feet 6 inches by 12 feet; S R, store-room, 4 by 12 feet.

DESIGN CX.

French Suburban Residence.

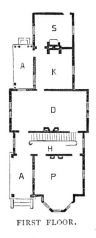

FIRST FLOOR.

SECOND FLOOR.

DESIGN CXI.

ITALIAN VILLA.

This Italian villa, constructed of brick, rubbed down and painted, will cost between $4500 and $5000, and if built of frame considerably less. The roof is of tin. The arrangement of steps to the principal floor has a good effect. The basement should be rubble masonry, pointed; the design shows the garden front, the principal front not being seen. The arrangement of the terraces, with flowering borders, will be most beautiful and unique. The situation of the fountain, both in front and rear, has a good effect. The terrace steps can be made of wood. This design is most admirably adapted to a summer seat.

The placing of vases and statues in front will be in beautiful harmony with the building. The front lawn should be kept broad, and not chopped up by foliage, and with very few plants in the ground. A line of jardinieres on each side of the principal walks, with a few solitary evergreens, properly situated, would carry out the effect.

First Floor.—H, hall; P, parlor, 14 by 20 feet; L, library, 15 by 15 feet; D R, dining-room, 12 by 18 feet; S R, sitting-room, 12 by 14 feet; D W, dumb-waiter; C, china-closet.

Second Floor.—H, hall; P C, principal chamber, 14 by 20 feet; C, chamber, 15 by 15 feet; C, chamber, 12 by 18 feet; N, nursery, 12 by 14 feet.

DESIGN CXI.

Italian Villa.

FIRST FLOOR.

SECOND FLOOR.

DESIGN CXII.

SUBURBAN OR COUNTRY RESIDENCE.

THIS design is for a cheap and commodious country or suburban residence. It is built of frame, with horizontal, narrow weather-boards. The window-frames have plank faces cut to the shape shown. It should have inside shutters throughout, and can be built with shingle or slate roof. The attic may contain servants' and store room, and provision is made for a cellar under the whole. Where it is possible to have houses in accordance with the nature of the ground, they are much more healthy and durable, and always repay their cost. This house can either be set with the broad side to the front, or the left-hand side can be front where the lot is narrower than sixty feet in front. The design has a plain, substantial appearance, but all its beauty will rest in the due weight and the proportion of its parts, and it must be treated to suit the location and its surroundings. It will make a very comfortable country or river-side house, but if the latter, the broad side should face the river. The plans are fully explained by their separate descriptions. The first story is twelve feet in the clear, the second ten feet, but they can be made higher. The house will cost to erect in the neighborhood of Philadelphia $8000 at this time.

First Floor.—V, porch; P, parlor, 14 by 20 feet; S, sitting-room, 12 by 12 feet; D, dining-room, 12 by 22 feet; K, kitchen, 12 by 12 feet; H, hall.

Second Floor.—C, chamber, 14 by 20 feet; B R, bath-room, 6 by 8 feet; B C, chamber, 12 by 20 feet; B, B, bed-rooms, 12 by 12 feet.

DESIGN CXII.

Suburban or Country Residence.

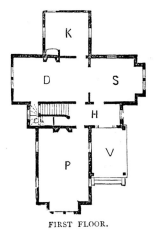

FIRST FLOOR.

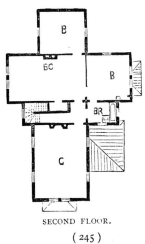

SECOND FLOOR.

(245)

DESIGN CXIII.

SUBURBAN RESIDENCE.

THIS was designed and built for Robert F. Lee, Esq., Pottsville, Pa., and has given much satisfaction. It is esteemed by many as being the most beautiful house in the city, and is situated upon high ground and set some distance back from the street. The grounds are nicely arranged, and the building is what may be called a plain square house with a kitchen wing thrown out on its rear. A bay end gives a beautiful effect upon entéring the parlor. The chimney being in the bay, with the aid of a large mantel-glass causes the doors of the parlor to be seen upon entering, as well as a beautiful chandelier, which gives the appearance of double the extent. The music-room, attached by sliding doors, can be thrown into one room, and the wide folding doors in the hall utilize the space and render the whole quite commodious and compact when closed. Much beauty, convenience, and comfort are sacrificed continually by persons building without securing these most important considerations.

First Floor.—P, porch; V, vestibule; H, hall, 8 feet wide; P, parlor, 19 by 24 feet; S R, sitting-room, 16 by 19 feet; D R, dining-room, 14 by 18 feet; M R, music-room, 10 by 14 feet; H R, rear hall, 6 feet wide; K, kitchen, 14 by 18 feet; S, scullery, 10 by 11 feet; P, pantry; C, closet, boiler inclosed.

Second Floor.—D R, dressing-room, 8 by 9 feet; P C, principal chamber, 19 by 19 feet; C, chamber, 14 by 19 feet; C, chamber, 14 by 15 feet; C, chamber, 14 by 17 feet; B R, bath-room, 7 by 8 feet; N, nursery, 12 by 18 feet; B R, bed-room, 10 by 13 feet; S R, store-room; C, C, clothes-presses.

DESIGN CXIII.

Suburban Residence.

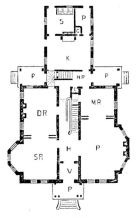

FIRST FLOOR.

SECOND FLOOR.

(247)

DESIGN CXIV.

SWISS COTTAGE.

THIS design of a Swiss cottage is organized to suit the American needs in some of our mountain glens and cañons of California. In such a situation it will have a very picturesque effect. It is one of those kinds of designs that are capable of being built of unplaned lumber, simply planed on the edges and cut to definite shapes, according to the design, and covered with shingles. It has a balcony half-way around the building, which screens the first story from sun and rain and renders the rooms comfortable, and acts as a wind sail, inducing air through the rooms in summer time. It is designed to be built of stone for first story, and brick for the second, with stone dressings, and will cost about $5000. It is necessary that full drawings should be secured with all parts clearly specified, that no more material shall be secured than the amount required, as the transportation in some localities costs more than the material. Terra-cotta chimney can be substituted for brick, as the weight is less and the cost less than bricks. A rough house built in this manner can have all the comforts, and in these situations be more beautiful than smooth-finished structures, and suit the taste of those who inhabit these localities. Porches, bays, etc., can be added to such a structure, and the whole building be ornamental in its shapes; the best architecture is possible. This building will cost about $3000, well built, in most sections of the country.

First Floor.—H, hall, 8 feet; P, parlor, 14 by 18 feet; S R, sitting-room, 11 by 14 feet; D R, dining-room, 20 by 14 feet; L, library, 11 by 14 feet; K, kitchen, 11 by 14 feet; W, wood-shed, 9 by 14 feet.

Second Floor.—C, chamber, 16 feet 6 inches by 14 feet; C, chamber, 11 by 14 feet; C, chamber, 12 by 14 feet; C, chamber, 8 by 14 feet; C, chamber, 11 by 14 feet; C, chamber, 10 feet 6 inches by 11 feet; with a bath-room 6 by 8 feet, and a large number of closets.

DESIGN CXIV.

Swiss Cottage.

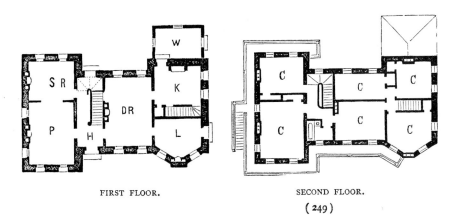

FIRST FLOOR.   SECOND FLOOR.

(249)

DESIGN CXV.

AMERICAN COTTAGE.

This design was organized for Mrs. Stabler, of Lynchburg, Va. It contains many desirable points, architecturally, and when constructed will be a bright and beautiful home, containing internally all modern improvements. It is designed to be built of bricks, hollow walls; the sash frames will have our new method of hanging them. They are so superior to the old method that our customers order them to be in their buildings. All the rattling of sash, and cold and dusty windows are prevented by the introduction of them. Parties building without the aid of an architect, and desiring detail drawings with the privilege of using this sash, would do well to obtain the same, which are furnished at a small figure. The building will cost, when finished, between $5000 and $6000.

First Floor.—A, parlor, 18 by 18 feet; B, hall; C, chamber, 18 by 20 feet; D, dining-room, 18 by 18 feet; E, smoking-room, 13 by 13 feet; F, nursery, 16 feet 6 inches by 23 feet; G, kitchen, 14 feet 6 inches by 14 feet; H, bath-room, 6 by 6 feet; I, store-room, 10 feet by 4 feet 3 inches; J, china-closet, 4 feet by 4 feet 3 inches.

Second Floor.—L, chambers; M, sewing-room.

DESIGN CXV.

American Cottage.

FIRST FLOOR.

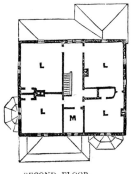

SECOND FLOOR.

DESIGN CXVI.

SUBURBAN RESIDENCE.

THIS design is one of those that meet with more admirers in this country than any other class of buildings. We send throughout the North, South, East and West, perhaps twenty similar designed buildings in a year, of this type, varied in their evolutions to suit different grounds and surroundings; also different plans, the number of rooms, closets, etc., are made to suit circumstances; also changes for different kinds of materials to be used in the construction, some of wood, as the above, others pointed stone, others brick, painted. The beauty rests in the proportions and treatment. The house can be built, completely finished, with all the modern improvements, hot and cold water, heater, and gas pipes throughout, for from $4000 to $7000, according to the expensive character of the materials used.

First Floor.—A, parlor, 12 by 18 feet; B, porch; D, office, 15 by 15 feet; R, kitchen, 12 by 13 feet 6 inches; F, dining-room, 15 by 12 feet.

Second Floor.—C, principal chamber, 12 by 18 feet; H, chamber, 15 by 12 feet; P, chamber, 10 by 12 feet; N, chamber, 15 by 15 feet.

DESIGN CXVI.

Suburban Residence.

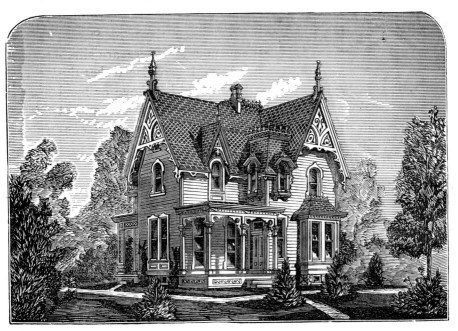

FIRST FLOOR.

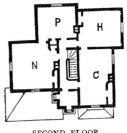

SECOND FLOOR.

DESIGN CXVII.

MODEL COTTAGE.

THIS model cottage, treated in the French chateau style, is one of those styles that will make a beautiful lone house admirably adapted to some situations. The house is intended to be built of stone, as high as the principal floor; above that of bricks, rubbed down and painted. The kitchen department and dining-room are in the basement. There are situations where such a house could be so placed that the approaches to the basement could be above or level with the grounds, and, by terraces, form beautiful broken grounds. This house will also stand a considerable amount of shrubbery. The design can be built, fully carried out with all its details complete, for $5000. But to make its ornaments thin and cheap, and make a pasteboard show of it, and finish it throughout in the same spirit, would require about $2500, with heater, gas, and water accommodations. In the article of plumbing alone it may cost $600 or $200. The mantels may cost $400 or $75. Heaters may cost $600 or $200. So throughout a house, good work and materials always cost more. We find in some localities that contractors differ very largely in their estimates. The following are the dimensions:

First Floor.—D R, dining-room, 18 feet 6 inches by 21 feet; K, kitchen, 12 by 13 feet; C C, china-closets, 5 by 6 feet; A, coal cellar, 11 by 12 feet; D, pantry, 6 feet 6 inches by 5 feet 6 inches; E, conservatory, 8 feet 6 inches by 10 feet.

Second Floor.—P, parlor, 18 feet 6 inches by 21 feet; C, chamber, 13 feet 6 inches by 11 feet 12 inches; B, bath-room, 5 feet 6 inches by 8 feet 6 inches; G, principal chamber, 12 by 13 feet.

DESIGN CXVII.

Model Cottage.

FIRST FLOOR.

SECOND FLOOR.

DESIGN CXVIII.

SUBURBAN RESIDENCE.

THIS design is intended for a residence in Kansas City, Mo. It is to be constructed of bricks, laid flush, joints rubbed down and painted. The trimmings around the windows, as sills and heads, are to be made of sandstone; also the elevation, as high as the principal floor. The porches and cornices are to be made of wood or galvanized iron; the roof of ornamental laid slates, but of one color. The glass used in the windows is of the first quality, double thick American. The interior is to be finished on the first and second floors in chestnut and walnut, with mantels, heaters, range, hot and cold water tank, lift pump, etc., as is usual in such houses. It will be complete in all its parts, and will cost, if built of brick, $8082, if built of frame, $6735, at the present cost of materials. The first story is twelve feet, and the second ten feet in the clear.

First Floor.—V, vestibule, 4 by 7 feet; H, stair-hall, 27 feet 6 inches by 20 feet 6 inches; P, parlor, 15 feet 6 inches by 25 feet, full length, including projecting window; D R, dining-room, 19 feet 6 inches by 15 feet 6 inches; S R, sitting-room, 12 by 17 feet; K, kitchen, 14 by 17 feet; Pan, pantry and store-room, 6 by 6 feet; it has also a china-closet from back stair-hall; the kitchen has a sink, circulating boiler, and range with fire-back, also a fine dresser; porches and cellar-doors outside, etc.

Second Floor has four chambers of the following dimensions:—the front chamber is 23 feet by 15 feet; the one over the kitchen is 15 feet 6 inches by 10 feet 6 inches; the one over the dining-room, 19 feet 6 inches by 15 feet 6 inches; a small room in the tower, 8 feet 6 inches by 6 feet.

DESIGN CXVIII.

Suburban Residence.

FIRST FLOOR.

SECOND FLOOR.

(257)

DESIGN CXIX.

CHILDREN'S HOME.

THIS design is of French Gamber, and was drawn for and the building is being erected by the Commissioners of Scioto County, Ohio. Such designs are organized entirely for utility and usefulness. No extraneous appendages are added but what become necessary. The building is treated in the highest art of proportion by suitable ornamental shapes; by this process, which is entirely American in spirit, parties have given us the credit of introducing simplicity and common sense in architectural structures. The practice of ancient and some modern architects, of adding string-courses, colonnades, false windows, chimneys, projecting piers, balustrades, etc., for simple ornament, without a particle of use, appears cowardly, expensive, and frivolous, when viewed by intelligence of the highest order, for whatever is seen in any building that does but deceive the person in regard to utility in its structure is a deficiency in sense and a lack of the highest principles in art, except in monumental work, which, like poetry, conforms to rules not admissible in prose. The engraving gives a fair representation of the building, but lacks that elegance and breadth that the finished structure will have. It will cost $25,000.

Ground Plan.—A, servants' sitting-room, 15 feet 6 inches by 24 feet; B, B, play-rooms, 15 feet 6 inches by 24 feet, 16 by 23 feet 6 inches; C, laundry, 18 by 18 feet; D, drying-room, 8 by 18 feet; E, bake-house, 20 by 20 feet; F, pantry, 9 by 15 feet 6 inches; G, kitchen, 20 by 24 feet; H, dining-room, 16 by 40 feet; a lavatory, 9 feet 6 inches by 16 feet; one water-closet.

First Floor.—K, parlor, 16 by 24 feet; L, matron's parlor, 16 by 24 feet; M, M, school-rooms, 18 by 24 feet, 20 feet 6 inches by 30 feet; N, N, sitting-rooms, 16 by 25 feet, 16 by 24 feet; O, sewing-room, 16 by 25 feet; P, chapel, 20 feet 6 inches by 24 feet; Q, matron's room, 8 feet 6 inches by 17 feet.

DESIGN CXIX.

Children's Home.

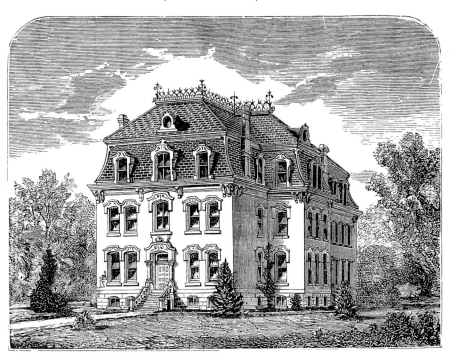

GROUND PLAN.

FIRST FLOOR.

DESIGN CXX.

CARRIAGE–HOUSE AND STABLE.

THIS was designed and built for Mr. Robbins, of Merchantville, N. J.,—distant three miles from Camden. It is very successful and beautiful.

Description of Diagram.—D, E, H, and K, box stalls, 11 by 14 feet 6 inches; F and G, open stalls, 5 by 8 feet 6 inches; C, harness-room; A, covered shed; B, open space.

This design, together with the one on page 98 (No. XXXIX.), will produce a beautiful combination. The plan, as will be seen by the diagram, is a first-class arrangement,—the stalls being of that particular kind known to horsemen as "box-stalls." They are four in number; and there are also two open stalls, with ample room for carriages.

DESIGN CXX.

Carriage-House and Stable.

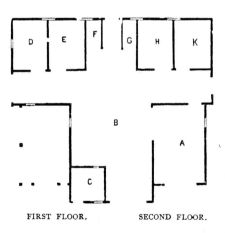

FIRST FLOOR.　　SECOND FLOOR.

DESIGN CXXI.

CEMETERY ENTRANCE.

THIS design is an evolution of the Ovo law of architecture. It was designed and built for a cemetery entrance in Lancaster City, Pennsylvania. The building is of brick, with rubbed sandstone dressings. The design was fully carried out in front, but was left plain in rear for economy. Professionally, we must say that, for its clear proportion, quiet, and unobtrusive beauty and fitness for its purpose, we have never seen so small a piece of architecture, costing so little money, contain half of its quiet, silent, reverential beauty.

This order possesses greater scope and is more in feeling with that which Christianity, through the development of the present human mind, is understood to teach,—a high morality, a refined and rounded culture, a quiet and temperate feeling, with a love for all that is pure and good. Lines discordant, harsh, and severe, are not in harmony with its rounded sentiments.

The basement consists of a central carriage-drive, 15 feet wide, on one side an office, 10 feet 5 inches by 18 feet; a stair-hall and stairway, 10 feet 6 inches by 12 feet; a receiving-vault, 10 feet 5 inches by 13 feet 9 inches, properly ventilated; upon the opposite side is a flagged paved passage, 10 feet 5 inches wide, with a stairway leading to the chapel, which is 36 feet by 48 feet 9 inches deep, fitted with plain, neat pews. The whole structure cost $10,000, and is a highly ornamental object. This must be considered quite a plain evolution of the order, which is capable of being made more ornate than any other existing style or order of architecture.

DESIGN CXXI.

Cemetery Entrance.

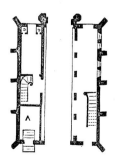
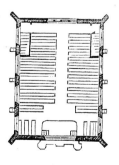

DESIGN CXXII.

MEMORIAL ARCHITECTURE.

THIS is the Centennial order of architecture. The base or platform upon which the columns rest is to be sculptured with Indian devices, the Landing of Columbus, etc. C, the base of columns, or plinth, represents the nations holding possession of portions of the Continent, and represented by their coat of arms, upon which rests a star-pointed shaft with thirteen points, representing the thirteen original States which formed the confederacy, each point capped with a star above. This is a shaft of thirty-seven points, representing the growth of the country.

The capital is ornamented with leaves and flowers of the century-plant, marking by its bloom the one hundred years, with the head of the Goddess of Liberty in bas-relief; above this is the entablature, ornamented with cannon-balls in bas-relief; with leaves and bloom of the century-plant. The whole capped with century-plants in full bloom, the stock answering for a flag-pole, from which waves the Star-Spangled Banner. The drawing is shown one-half in section, the other in elevation; the distance between is the intercolumniation of the order. The proportion is extracted from a well-informed American man.

DESIGN CXXII.

Memorial Architecture.

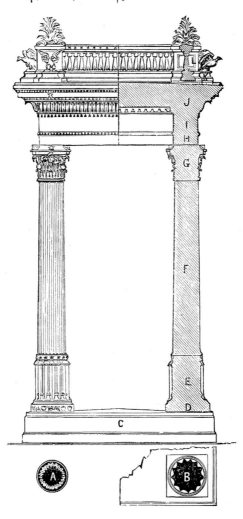